Taoist Shaman

Fu Hsi (Fu See) Hermit Sage
Author of the I Ching

Taoist Shaman

Practices from
the Wheel of Life

Mantak Chia and
Kris Deva North

Destiny Books
Rochester, Vermont • Toronto, Canada

Destiny Books
One Park Street
Rochester, Vermont 05767
www.DestinyBooks.com

Destiny Books is a division of Inner Traditions International

Originally published in Thailand in 2009 by Universal Healing Tao Publications
under the title *The Taoist Medicine Wheel: Tao of the Shaman Book 1*

Library of Congress Cataloging-in-Publication Data
Chia, Mantak, 1944–
  Taoist Shaman : practices from the wheel of life / Mantak Chia and Kris Deva
North.
    p. cm.
  Includes bibliographical references and index.
  ISBN 978-1-59477-365-5 (pbk.)
  1. Taoism. 2. Shamanism. I. North, Kris Deva. II. Title. III. Title: Practices
from the wheel of life.
  BL1923.C5365 2010
  299.5'14—dc22

                                                              2010032029

Printed and bound in Canada

10 9 8 7 6 5 4 3 2

Text design by Priscilla Baker
Text layout by Virginia Scott Bowman
This book was typeset in Jansen Text with Present as the display typeface

Contents

Acknowledgments

The Universal Tao Publications staff involved in the preparation and production of *Taoist Shaman* extend our gratitude to the many generations of Taoist masters who have passed on their special lineage, in the form of an unbroken oral transmission, over thousands of years. We thank Taoist Master Yi Eng for his openness in transmitting the formulas of Taoist Inner Alchemy. We also wish to thank the thousands of unknown men and women of the Chinese healing arts who developed many of the methods and ideas presented in this book.

We offer our eternal gratitude to our parents and teachers for their many gifts to us. Remembering them brings joy and satisfaction to our continued efforts in presenting the Universal Tao System. For their gifts, we offer our eternal gratitude and love. As always, their contribution has been crucial in presenting the concepts and techniques of the Universal Tao.

For their efforts to clarify the text and produce this handsome new edition of the book, we thank the editorial and production staff at Inner Traditions/Destiny Books. We also thank Nancy Yeilding for her line edit of the new edition.

We wish to thank the following people for their assistance in producing the original edition of this book: Vinod Solluna for his editorial work, Hirunyathorn Punsan for his graphic design work, Anamarta for photography, Juan Li for his color illustrations, and Kris Deva North for the shamanic diagrams.

A special thanks goes to our Thai production team: Raruen

Keawapadung, computer graphics, and Saniem Chaisarn, production designer.

Kris Deva North wishes to thank his shamanic teachers, the Wakamba, especially Mwala Ibuti and Nethenge Ngube, Wakan of the Banjalong, Kumbahadur Gurung, Rowan Saille, Samara Hawthorn; Wa-Na-Ne-Che of the Lakota; Howard Wills; Rene Navarro for the original reading list.

To Alexander West for Amazonian insights; Matt Lewis and adepts of the London Universal Healing Tao Center for allowing themselves to be guinea pigs in testing arcane techniques of Taoist ecstasy; the Grimstone Community 1999 to 2007 for their annual tolerance of the Din of Death.

To Guillaume Bouteloup for permission to excerpt his thesis "Uses of the I Ching;" John Mark Eggerton for permission to use "Calling the Directions"; Dr. Sandra Goodman of *Positive Health* magazine for permission to excerpt "Calabash of Light"; Esther Jantzen for her notes on Howard Wills; Vinod Solluna for his contribution on the Western Dragon Tradition; and Anamarta for her love, support, patience, and inspiration.

Putting Taoist Shamanic Techniques into Practice

The practices described in this book have been used successfully for thousands of years by Taoists trained by personal instruction. Readers should not undertake the practice without receiving personal transmission and training from a certified instructor of the Universal Tao, since certain of these practices, if done improperly, may cause injury or result in health problems. This book is intended to supplement individual training by the Universal Tao and to serve as a reference guide for these practices. Anyone who undertakes these practices on the basis of this book alone does so entirely at his or her own risk.

The meditations, practices, and techniques described herein are not intended to be used as an alternative or substitute for professional medical treatment and care. Any reader suffering from illnesses based on psychological or emotional disorders should consult an appropriate professional health care practitioner or therapist. Such problems should be corrected before you start training.

This book does not attempt to give any medical diagnosis, treatment, prescription, or remedial recommendation in relation to any human disease, ailment, suffering, or physical condition whatsoever.

The Universal Tao cannot be responsible for the consequences of any practice or misuse of the information in this book. If the reader undertakes any exercise without strictly following the instructions, notes, and warnings, the responsibility must lie solely with the reader.

Taoist Shamanic Tradition—from Mystery to History

When human beings first stood upon the land and looked about the horizon they saw in the distance around them the edge of a mystic circle where Heaven above touched Earth below. Moving about within that circle, they noticed certain constants:

- Wherever each moved, his or her place was always at the center, between Heaven and Earth.
- For each one it was the same, and so for each one different.
- The sun always rose from one point in that circle and set in another, and then Heaven darkened until lit by stars, or an inconstant moon.
- Whereas the sun moved across Heaven by day, by night Heaven moved around one star, which remained fixed and constant.
- For each one it was the same, and so the same for all, wherever humans moved on Earth.

Thus the ancient humans discovered that each of one of us is the center of our own universe, while Heaven has its own center. They observed the power of Heaven, seeing that the fire of Heaven warms and illuminates Earth, that water falls from Heaven to Earth, lightning splits Heaven and strikes Earth while Heaven rumbles, and wind rushes between Heaven and Earth. Heaven commands Earth. Thus whoever has Heaven's mandate rules Earth.

The shaman kings began as leaders talking to Heaven. One story says that a group of Aryans shipwrecked on the China shore thousands of years ago did not die, nor have children; they became known as the Shining Ones. They taught shamanic practices, including the protective circle, calling the elements, ecstatic journeying and flight, power animals, and tutelary deities or guides.

From Yu, the legendary son of the bear—shape-shifter, sky-dancer, and traveler in the underworld—right down through the Western Chou Dynasty (1122–770 BCE), shamans continued to follow the bear, wearing bearskin robes in ceremony. Their power dwindled in succeeding years; by the end of the Eastern Chou (221 BCE), when warring states were unified under the Ch'in, many shamanic traditions had been absorbed into schools of Taoism (fig. 1.1). When the Ch'in dynasty embraced Confucianism over Taoism, shamanism went underground.

Shamanic influence was restored at court under the Western Han (206 BCE–8 CE) as religious and magical Taoism, especially of the Fang Shih, who developed Inner Alchemy and Feng Shui. The next dynasty, however, the Eastern Han (25–220 CE), saw the last of the court shamans replaced by scholars and civil servants. The simple philosophy, or Tao Chia, expounded by Lao-tzu in the Tao Te Ching around 600 BCE had become Tao Chiao, religious dogma, by second century of the first millennium. The "Do-It-Yourself" principles of Taoism were competing with Confucianism's reassuringly strict codes of behavior for all situations. But in villages of the countryside, the "old ways" and their practitioners still held sway, evolving Taoism as a folk religion of mystery and secrecy, with rites, rituals, and initiations. Families and priests, sources of the great schools of Taoism with their ideological and geographical differences, practiced shamanic Taoism as local cults.

Chang Tao-ling (34–156 CE), a Fang Shih, traveled in western

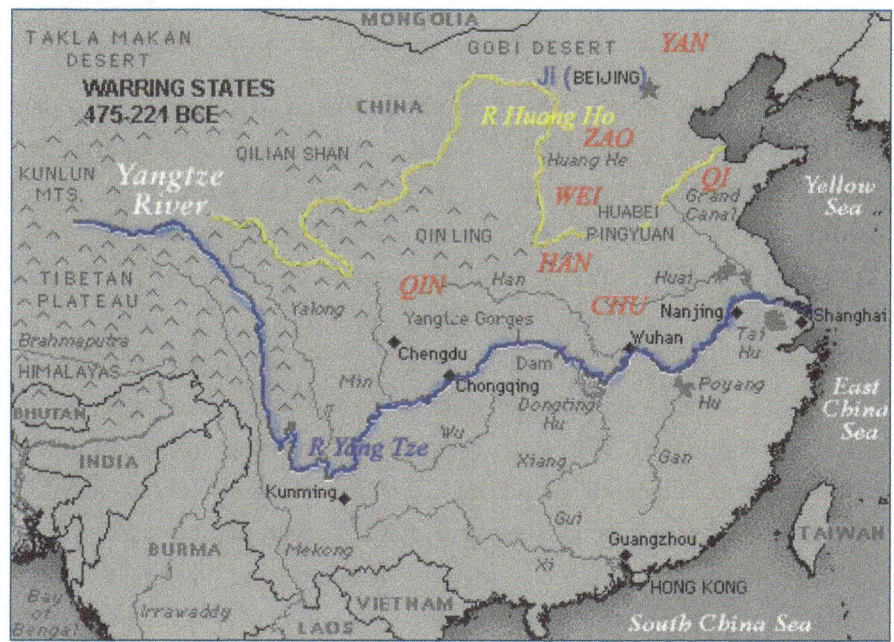

Fig. 1.1. During the Warring States period in China, 475–221 BCE,
seven states vied for supremacy.

China (now Sichuan/Yunnan), a remote part of the kingdom where
shamanism was still widely practiced. Influenced by Tibetan Tantric
practices, Chang founded the school Seven Bushels of Rice, which
evolved into the Celestial Masters. In the following centuries their
fortunes rose and fell with changing dynasties and conflicts between
Taoist, Confucian, and Buddhist doctrines.

In 265 CE, under the Eastern Ch'in, the Lady Wei, daughter of
a Celestial Masters' priest and herself a priestess, founded the Shang
ch'ing school of Taoists to revive and sustain the shamanic practices
of ecstatic flight and journeying. Tao Hung-ching, a former librarian
at Court, collected and collated Shang ch'ing scripts, including the I
Ching, wrote and practiced Inner Alchemy, and founded the monas-
tery on Mount Maoshan, still there today.

In the Northern Wei Dynasty (386–534 CE), K'ou Ch'ien-chih
established a branch of the Celestial Masters inspired by puritanical
Buddhist ideas of celibacy. With reforming zeal he instituted rules
and regulations attacking shamanic and sexual practices. In 420 CE
his version of Celestial Masters' Taoism was made state religion in the

north and persecution of the shamans followed. Thus it came to pass that the very refuge sought by the shamans became a place of hostility. However, they continued their practices in secret, without the use of drums, rattles, robes, or other articles of the craft to identify them. As the saying goes, "you cannot tell a sage by his clothes." They were also known as magicians, wizards, and sorcerers.

Over the centuries Taoism declined from state religion to fragmentation. The puritan reformation declined too and many texts on sexual practices reappeared. While the formal religious aspect was crumbling, scholars and officials fell in and out of favor in the political chaos. Many became hermits, practicing the naturalistic Taoism of Lao-tzu and integrating it with their Confucian ideas. A notice stating "There is an altar in this house" was a sign of a safe haven for the traveling Taoist during the Buddhist persecutions. The tradition has been maintained to this day to show the location of a Taoist household or temple.

Various scriptures were written, compiled, revised, lost, hidden, stolen, or burned according to the political and religious flavor of the times. During the Song period the Complete Clarity School sought to return to the simplicity of the original practice. Then the first Ming emperor—having overthrown the Yuan or Mongol dynasty in the fourteenth century with the help of the magician Liu Po-hun—appointed the Celestial Masters to lead the official state religion, which included magic and sorcery. In the twenty-first century, the sixty-third Celestial Master of the direct lineage lives in Taiwan.

TODAY'S SHAMAN

In ancient China, barefoot healers, pre-Taoist shamans wearing red headbands, wandered naked and were subject to fits, a characteristic particularly of the Siberian shamans but also known among shamans of other traditions. From these roots, Taoist shamanism persevered through the chaos of the warring states and later persecutions, and persisted through Taoism's rise to become the official religion of the Imperial dynasties and its subsequent decline.

Today the shaman is the healer in a community and, particularly in the Taoist tradition, is known only to the community, unknown in the outer world. This secrecy stems from the days of persecution. As a healing warrior, the shaman mediates with, or combats, Spirit, by taking into her- or himself the energies to heal and to seal. As "mediator with Spirit" the shaman is chosen by Spirit and called by humans when other healing practices such as herbs, massage, acupuncture, or allopathy have failed. If sickness prevails, the shaman finds out from Spirit what healing the soul needs for the body to be whole again. The shaman enlivens the perspective that everything is a gift and a blessing, for everything is love, and gratitude and thanks must be given even for hurt and pain. Then harmony can be restored between soul and body.

However, practitioners of shamanism can be susceptible to suffering afflictions of Spirit in this earthly dimension. I personally know two people—one an acknowledged practitioner and the other a young boy recognized by his teachers as having shamanic power—who have an extremely difficult time living in the "normal" world themselves but are able to help others through their Spirit connection. This, of course, is where modern-day Taoist practitioners have the advantage of the Healing Tao system to protect themselves from depletion and contamination.

Taoism recommends all of the following to help you gain a deeper understanding of self, your connection with community, and your harmony with all the different forces around you. Create your own path, for you are your own creation.

- Spiritual development
- Meditation
- Chi Kung
- Tai Chi
- Understanding the forces of nature and your own true nature
- Understanding the spirit of the animals and the way of nature

The Taoist medicine wheel and the practices that go with it integrate the insights of all these approaches.

The Taoist Medicine Wheel

Peering into the misted past to peel away the shroud of mystery, we open the secret archives of the Chinese diaspora, where the traditions of the Tao were guarded until its resurgence in the New Age. We humans are curious animals, inquisitive creatures who like things explained. Before we had the means of measuring or scientific explanation, we sat around fires or huddled in caves after some natural disaster and tried to explain it. Imagine a world changed by great Earth-moving and Heaven-rending

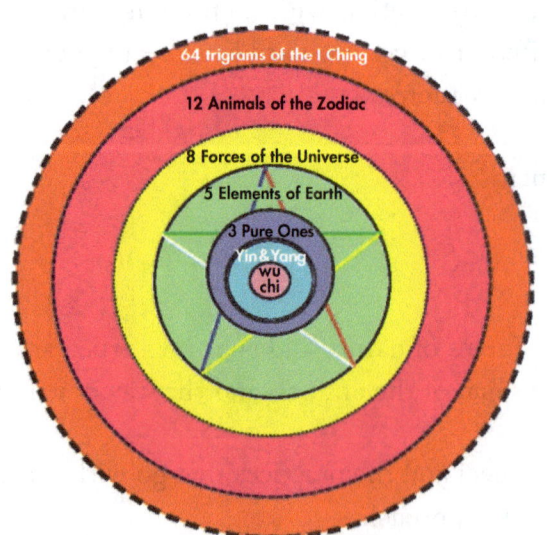

Fig. 2.1. The Taoist Medicine Wheel

events such as earthquakes, lightning, storms, and floods. Plausible explanations and stories spread and legends grew as families evolved into clans, tribes became states, and kingdoms became an empire.

In one Taoist myth of creation, the universe began as an egg from which hatched the primeval human, Pan Go. The light parts of the shell floated up to form Heaven, the heavier parts fell to form Earth. Pan Go stood erect, arms supporting Heaven and feet holding Earth in place.

In another myth the Tao began the moment fire fused with water. Before that there was only emptiness, Wu Chi. From that Original Source, referred to as the One, developed the two aspects of the universe that have become popular buzzwords for the past four decades in the West: yin and yang. When lightning struck the sea, the yang of fire entered the yin of water, and life began. The two of yin and yang gave birth to the Three Pure Ones, which begat the five elements and the ten thousand things.

The Taoist sages saw the medicine wheel as a representation of all creation, including Wu Chi, the Three Pure Ones, the principles of yin and yang, the five elements, the eight forces of the universe, the twelve power animals of the Chinese zodiac, and the sixty-four trigrams of the I Ching (fig. 2.1). The Taoist medicine wheel is the foundation of most Chinese art, of the traditional Chinese medicines we know today as acupuncture and herbalism, of Chinese astrology and divination, of Tai Chi Chuan, "the supreme ultimate" combining meditation and martial art, and of the esoteric sexual practices taught to the emperors by their female advisers to form the basis of Taoist alchemy: the quest for immortality.

The core of the wheel is Wu Chi (see fig. 2.2 on page 8), the circle denoting emptiness or readiness. It can be understood in the healing and martial arts as the empty mind that is the beginning of response, readiness to respond to a condition or to an opponent's action; in art as the blank sheet awaiting the artist's inspiration in words or pictures; in meditation as entering the void. It is like the empty stage of a spiritual theater, awaiting the players, words, or images.

The next layer is the interplay of yin and yang within the circle, yin becoming yang, yang becoming yin, which denotes the change that is life from its broadest scale to its microcosmic alternation between wave and particle (fig. 2.3).

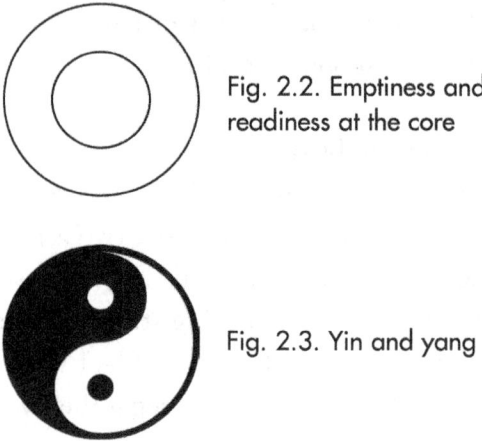

Fig. 2.2. Emptiness and readiness at the core

Fig. 2.3. Yin and yang

The Three Treasures or Pure Ones—universal or heavenly chi, higher-self or cosmic chi, and earth chi—are contained within the yin/yang symbol. Traditionally, the Three Pure Ones were visualized as three emperors residing in the three palaces or centers of the body called the upper, middle, and lower *tan tiens*. The upper tan tien (which includes the third eye, the crown, and the entire head) connects to the universal chi through the force of *shen* or spirit.* The middle tan tien connects to the heart and other organs through the natural force of our soul, known as *chi*, which is both the life force and the organizing principle flowing through all things and establishing their interconnectedness. The lower tan tien (lower abdomen, centered between the navel and the kidneys) connects the physical body, the sexual energy,

---

Spirit in this sense means an individual's spirit rather than the Great Spirit, the Tao. At conception, when yin and yang collide in nuclear fusion, the personal spirit or life force begins. Throughout life, spirit can awaken and be allowed to nourish itself and grow; it can be awakened, nourished, and grown, or be left asleep, suppressed, or neglected. Like totems, guides, and guardians, spirit can seek another home or simply disappear into the cosmic soup. Personal spirit blends with Great Spirit at the ultimate level, reunion with the Tao.

Fig. 2.4. The five elements are depicted here as part of nature's creation cycle, proceeding from water, associated with winter, to wood, associated with spring, to fire, associated with summer, to earth, associated with Indian summer, to metal, associated with autumn.

and Mother Earth through the force known as *ching*, which gives cohesion to the physical aspect of life.

From the Three Pure Ones, the sages adduced the five elements governing life in this earthly dimension: fire, earth, metal, water, and wood (fig. 2.4). They are represented by a pentacle in the next layer of the wheel.

In the rich symbology of the Taoist cosmos, eight additional forces that influence human life are at play: heaven, earth, fire, water, wind, thunder, lake, and mountain. They are represented by the eight trigrams of the *pakua* (*pa* means "eight"; *kua* means "trigram"), which originated in the pattern of the turtle or tortoise shell used in prehistoric shamanic divination (see figs. 2.5 and 2.6 on page 10).

The lines on the turtle's back were thought to be a divine diagram corresponding to 1–8 (not 0–7) coded in binary, each placed as a side/corner of the compass diagram. From this shape evolved the drum and circle walking, which symbolized the change of seasons, from the early steps of the spring through blossoming summer, reaping life's harvest to sustain us into the autumn of retirement and cold winter of death.

Fig. 2.5. The eight trigrams were discovered in the pattern of the tortoise shell.

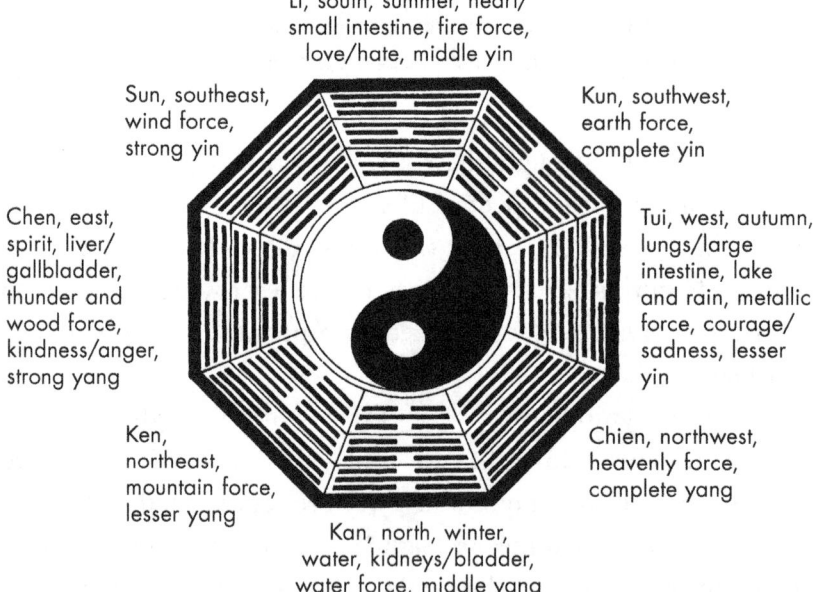

Li, south, summer, heart/small intestine, fire force, love/hate, middle yin

Sun, southeast, wind force, strong yin

Kun, southwest, earth force, complete yin

Chen, east, spirit, liver/gallbladder, thunder and wood force, kindness/anger, strong yang

Tui, west, autumn, lungs/large intestine, lake and rain, metallic force, courage/sadness, lesser yin

Ken, northeast, mountain force, lesser yang

Chien, northwest, heavenly force, complete yang

Kan, north, winter, water, kidneys/bladder, water force, middle yang

Fig. 2.6. The eight forces of the universe are depicted on the pakua (or bagua) as eight trigrams. In this arrangement of the trigrams, the trigram Kan, which is associated with the north, is at the bottom of the pakua and the trigram Li, which is associated with the south, is at the top. As you will see in chapter 4, the trigrams of the pakua are sometimes arranged in the opposite order. Chapter 6 shows yet another arrangement that places opposing elements opposite one another.

The twelve signs of the zodiac, derived from ancient totems, describe twelve basic personality types. Each is either yin or yang and each is associated with one of the five elements.

ANIMAL	YIN/YANG	ELEMENT
Rat	Yang	Water
Ox	Yin	Water
Tiger	Yang	Wood
Rabbit	Yin	Wood
Dragon	Yang	Wood
Snake	Yin	Fire
Horse	Yang	Fire
Sheep/Goat/Ram	Yin	Fire
Monkey	Yang	Metal
Rooster	Yin	Metal
Dog	Yang	Metal
Pig	Yin	Water

The eight trigrams combine to form the sixty-four hexagrams of the I Ching as the outer circle. (Chapter 6 will provide more detail on the I Ching.)

THE MEDICINE WHEEL IN DAILY LIFE

The body is a microcosm of the universe, in which the pointed bones are the earthly manifestation of stars and mountains, the hollows are lakes and ditches, the meridians (energy channels) are rivers, the organs are elements, and where our internal weather (health, emotional stability, spiritual harmony) are influenced by the heat, cold, and damp of Earth and the wind and thunder of Heaven.

Simple, but perhaps incomprehensible, is the concept of each human being as center of the universe, conceived in perfection of body, mind, and spirit, reflecting the karma of past lives of the self, ancestors, and descendants. At the moment of conception we sign our "contract with Heaven" for this life. Earth is the dimension in which we live in this incarnation. Unlike belief systems that see earthly life as suffering, or a "vale of tears," the Tao proclaims "all things and all experiences as innately perfect . . . sin is not recognized, nor any concept of right and wrong beyond individual conscience." Life is good! It is considered unnecessary to create difficult and painful processes. Pain and difficulties arise only from our responses to experiences, which can lead to variations on our contract, which in turn can lead to imbalances in the being, which can manifest as emotional disturbance and illness.

As we go through the seven phases of life, from infant to sage, we respond to situations in different ways, either returning to or moving away from the perfect state of our conception, the ultimate aim being to return to that prenatal Heaven, the Source. The medicine wheel offers us a way to enter different states at will, to "step lightly in all worlds." It is the circle of life, connecting the outer with the inner, the higher with lower. Uses of the medicine wheel abound in daily life: the five elements are helpful in generating energy, fusion of the eight forces offers wonderful meditations for clearing the spiritual path, the interplay between the twelve animals helps with understanding the self in relation to others, and the hexagrams aid in problem-solving. Before looking more deeply into shamanic practices, we will take a closer look at these aspects of the medicine wheel that form their foundation.

The Five Elements

The five elements refer to five basic energy transformations that flow from the interactions of yin and yang. The physical elements found in nature (wood, fire, earth, metal, and water) are seen as symbolic expressions of the five tendencies of energy in motion (see fig. 3.1 on page 14). Wood represents energy that is developing and generating. Fire represents energy that is expanding and radiating. Earth represents energy that is stabilizing and centering. Metal represents energy that is solidifying and contracting. Water is energy that is conserving, gathering, and sinking.

The five elements are related to the seasons. Spring sees the green budding of new life in plants and trees that bear fruit in the red heat of summer. Ripe yellow fields lie ready to reap before gray autumn sets in. Blue with cold in winter when water turns to ice, life goes indoors to die after conceiving anew for spring. So the seasons turn, under Heaven. The spirits of the seasons are the elements, ruling the human landscape as weather rules the mundane world.

What is fire like? What does it do? Fire warms and comforts,
  burns and destroys, dances like flame, cannot be grasped.
Earth is serene, balanced, earthy! Living with it, we don't notice
  it hurtling round the sun at thousands of miles an hour.
Metal is bright, hard, and sharp; it can cut and contain, reflect and

Fig. 3.1. These trees growing around rocks illustrate the elements of wood and metal.

inspire. And metal can be melted and shaped with warmth.
Water can be still or stormy, destructive or compliant. Water fits
into anything; it can turn to ice or steam, tears or tidal waves.
Wood has focus and direction, competes for light, and grows in
all directions.

Different aspects of the elements exert influences on one another,
some nourishing, some regulating. Their nourishing influences are
expressed as the "Cycle of Support," and their regulating influences
are expressed as "Lines of Control."

Elements Nourish One Another in the Cycle of Support

- The sun, fire, blesses earth
- Deep within earth, metal is born
- From the rock of metal springs water
- Water feeds plant life, wood
- And wood is the fuel for fire

Disturbances can happen; too much sun can scorch the earth, so
the springs run dry, or too little sun leaves crops unripened.

Elements Regulate One Another in the Lines of Control

- Fire melts metal
- Metal cuts wood
- Wood grips earth
- Earth directs water
- Water regulates fire

In life, full of surprises, metal sometimes refuses to melt, being too strong or the flame too weak; wood can blunt the ax; an eroded earth is too hard or crumbling for roots to grip; flash floods break the banks; too much fire evaporates water.

ELEMENTAL CORRESPONDENCES

In traditional Chinese medicine, the life-force energy of chi is seen to circulate through the human body through a series of channels or meridians. In addition to their correspondences with the seasons, the elements are also associated with particular meridians, which are named after the internal organs as they are described in traditional Chinese medicine. Altogether there are fourteen meridians that together form a cycle through which chi circulates over a period of twenty-four hours. During the course of a day each meridian will have a two-hour "period" when maximum energy is flowing through it.

Each organ meridian is designated as either yin or yang. Yin and yang are generally used to describe the relationships between things. For example, men are more yang and women more yin, but among both men and women are those more yin or yang in comparison with others of the same gender. Fire is more yang, water more yin, but a candle is more yin than the sun and a wave more yang than a tear drop. Yin meridians relate to inner aspects of the body and correspond with the deeper organs: heart, lungs, liver, spleen, and kidney. The yang channels relate to the outer aspects and network the more hollow organs: the intestines, bladder, and gallbladder. The yin meridians can be thought of as relating to the more inner, emotional, and spiritual aspects and the yang to the more physical and mundane.

TIMES OF MAXIMUM ENERGY FOR THE MERIDIANS	
MERIDIAN	**TIME**
Gall Bladder	11 p.m. to 1 a.m.
Liver	1 a.m. to 3 a.m.
Lungs	3 a.m. to 5 a.m.
Large Intestine	5 a.m. to 7 a.m.
Stomach	7 a.m. to 9 a.m.
Spleen	9 a.m. to 11 a.m.
Heart	11 a.m. to 1 p.m.
Small Intestine	1 p.m. to 3 p.m.
Bladder	3 p.m. to 5 p.m.
Kidneys	5 p.m. to 7 p.m.
Heart Protector/Pericardium	7 p.m. to 9 p.m.
Triple Heater	9 p.m. to 11 p.m.

Each element is also associated with a direction, a sense and sense organ, a color, a guardian animal, and positive and negative emotions.

South—Fire

Fire dances, fire warms, fire burns, fire creates, and fire destroys.

The sun shines, fire nourishing earth, nourished by wood, controlling metal, controlled by water.

Love is the virtue of fire energy in its positive aspect, while the negative emotion is impatience.

The sense of the fire element is the sense of taste, and the feature is the tongue.

The color of fire is red, its season is summer, and the guardian animal is the Firebird or Red Pheasant.

Meridians of the fire element are four: Heart, Small Intestine, Triple Heater, and Heart Protector, or Pericardium, each of which has a special role in the land of the living.

West—Metal

Metal reflects and inspires, cuts and contains; it is the element of mystery, of swords and shields, coins, boxes, and silver-backed mirrors. Ancient alchemists sought to transform base metal into gold.

Born in the depths of earth, metal nourishes water. Its sharp edge controls wood and is itself controlled by fire as in the blacksmith's forge.

Metal's virtue is boldness and its negative emotion is misery, with associations of loneliness, isolation, sadness, and depression, especially the sadness of loss or unrequited love.

The sense of the metal element is smell, thus the nose is the feature of metal.

The color of metal is white, the season is autumn, and the guardian animal is the White Tiger.

The yin meridian of metal is Lung and the yang is Large Intestine.

East—Wood

The wood element is the energy of birth, rebirth, and renewal, the unstoppability of life, the bursting of bud through bough. Wood energy is dynamic, competitive (sometimes to the point of aggression), and powerful. Little plants grow in the brick walls of buildings and trees uproot the pavements of city streets.

Wood (tree, plant life) is the element of movement in all directions: roots penetrate down into the earth, the trunk rises erect toward the heavens, and branches spread outward.

Trees compete for the light above and shade the earth below. Alive, they are nourished by water and their roots hold earth in place. They are cut by metal and provide fuel for fire.

Wood takes the conception energy of water and transforms it into lust for life: survival, sexual desire, or continuation of the species, and the need to grow or progress.

Kindness is the virtue of wood energy in its positive aspect, while the negative emotion is anger.

The sense of the wood element is the sense of sight, possibly our most powerful sense: 90 percent of our sensory input comes through our eyes.

The color of wood is green, the season is spring, and the guardian animal is the Dragon.

Wood's yin meridian is Liver and yang, Gall Bladder.

Center or Southwest—Earth

Earth is still. Earth is our Mother and provides all our needs. Everything we use comes from earth and requires only work to transform it into anything from a spaceship to a wheelbarrow.

Deep in earth metal is born. Earth supports water, is held in place by wood, and nourished by fire, as the sun shines on the earth, giving light and life.

Calmness is the virtue of earth energy in its positive aspect, while the negative emotion is worry.

The sense of the earth element is the sense of touch, and the feature is the mouth.

The color of earth is yellow, its season is harvest time when the fields are yellow and gold, and the guardian animal is the Golden Phoenix.

Meridians of the earth element are Stomach, yang, and Spleen, yin.

North—Water

Did life begin when lightning struck the ocean? If water holds the power of life, it can also carry the power of destruction. It was a flood that ended Noah's world.

Water is nature's shape-shifter, freezing solid as ice, boiling to steam, flowing as a teardrop or a tidal wave. As plain water it adapts to any shape, fits in any container, and, left to its own devices, always flows down to find the lowest level—a good thing to remember when "going with the flow."

Rivers flow into the ocean, which evaporates into clouds, which rain on the earth and refill the rivers. Water nourishes plant life, wood, and is nourished by the rocks of its sources, metal. Riverbanks and oceans are held in place by earth. And water controls fire, as you know from the barbecue and the fire brigade.

Water's virtues are gentleness and wisdom and its emotion fear.

The sense of the water element is the sense of hearing: the ears are the feature of water.

Water's color is blue, its season is winter, the time of death and conception. Water's guardian animals are the Turtle and the Deer.

Meridians of the water element are Kidney, yin, and Bladder, yang.

The shaman views each living being as a microcosm of these elemental energies, reflecting the universe and its interacting forces. Health and well-being are ruled by the interplay between them. Emotions such as anger, misery, fear, impatience, and worry occur through interaction between elements. Positive feelings of kindness, love, calm, courage, and gentleness nourish one another and regulate the negative emotions. Acting in a way that is contrary to our own nature can lead to imbalances in the elemental relationships within us and such distortions can result in a "condition" of dis-ease within a person. When such imbalances take place, the shaman can recognize which element might be bullying another, or which element might be too weak to stand up for itself. The shaman seeks to harmonize yin and yang within elements, organs, meridians, and points.

BEYOND ELEMENTS

The Taoist shaman masters reasoned that to become connected to the outer universe, they first needed to gain control of their own inner universe, which they experienced as a flow of energy, or chi, through their bodies. They discovered that, in addition to the organ-meridians, two parental meridians flow outside the elemental structure. Through the central energy centers (similar to yoga chakras) they offer direct contact with spirit and connection with the rest of the meridian network.

The Governor Vessel or Channel, the yang partner, connects the energy centers of the back; the Conception Vessel or Functional Channel, the yin meridian, connects those of the front (see figs. 3.2 and 3.3 on pages 21 and 22). When they are joined together, they form the body's major energy circuit, the Microcosmic Orbit.

 ## Basic Microcosmic Orbit Meditation

The Microcosmic Orbit meditation develops the power of the mind to control, conserve, recycle, transform, and direct energy through the body.

1. Join the Governor Channel with the Functional Channel to form the Microcosmic Orbit by touching your tongue to the roof of your mouth just behind your front teeth.

2. Begin in the eyes and allow your mind to circulate with the energy as it travels down the front of your body through your tongue, throat, chest, and navel and then up the tailbone and spine to the head. Feel the energy circulate through the Microcosmic Orbit by letting your mind flow along with it.

Fusion of the Five Elements Practice

The Taoist practice of Internal Alchemy begins with Fusion of the Five Elements, which focuses on the interaction and fusion of all five elements and their correspondences, and their transformation into a harmonious whole of high-quality energy. During this process, the

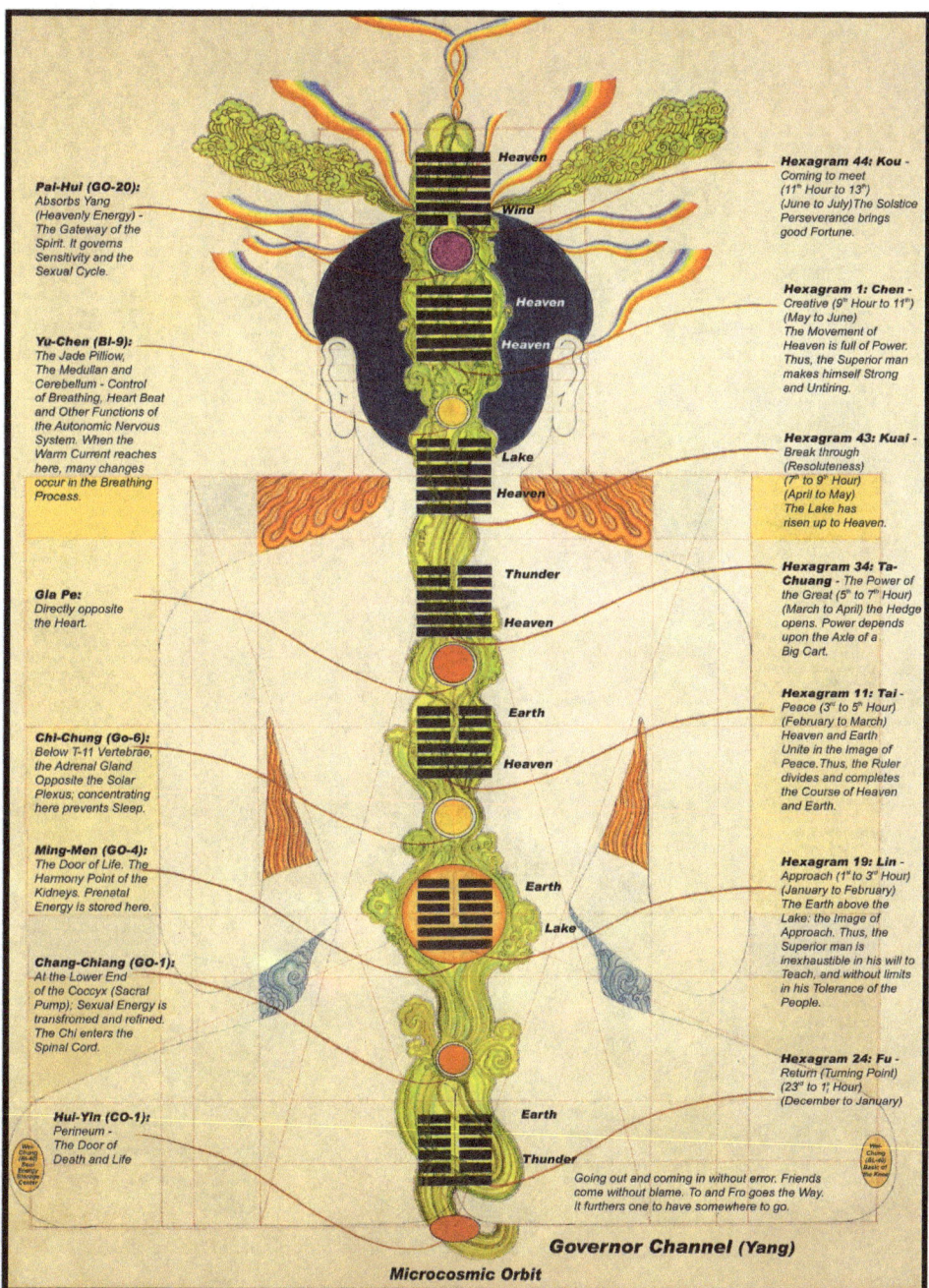

Pai-Hui (GO-20):
Absorbs Yang
(Heavenly Energy) -
The Gateway of the
Spirit. It governs
Sensitivity and the
Sexual Cycle.

Yu-Chen (BI-9):
The Jade Pillow,
The Medullan and
Cerebellum - Control
of Breathing, Heart Beat
and Other Functions of
the Autonomic Nervous
System. When the
Warm Current reaches
here, many changes
occur in the Breathing
Process.

Gia Pe:
Directly opposite
the Heart.

Chi-Chung (Go-6):
Below T-11 Vertebrae,
the Adrenal Gland,
Opposite the Solar
Plexus; concentrating
here prevents Sleep.

Ming-Men (GO-4):
The Door of Life. The
Harmony Point of the
Kidneys. Prenatal
Energy is stored here.

Chang-Chiang (GO-1):
At the Lower End
of the Coccyx (Sacral
Pump); Sexual Energy is
transfromed and refined.
The Chi enters the
Spinal Cord.

Hui-Yin (CO-1):
Perineum -
The Door of
Death and Life

Heaven
Wind
Heaven
Heaven
Lake
Heaven
Thunder
Heaven
Earth
Heaven
Earth
Lake
Earth
Thunder

Hexagram 44: Kou -
Coming to meet
(11ᵗʰ Hour to 13ᵗʰ)
(June to July) The Solstice
Perseverance brings
good Fortune.

Hexagram 1: Chen -
Creative (9ᵗʰ Hour to 11ᵗʰ)
(May to June)
The Movement of
Heaven is full of Power.
Thus, the Superior man
makes himself Strong
and Untiring.

Hexagram 43: Kuai -
Break through
(Resoluteness)
(7ᵗʰ to 9ᵗʰ Hour)
(April to May)
The Lake has
risen up to Heaven.

Hexagram 34: Ta-
Chuang - The Power of
the Great (5ᵗʰ to 7ᵗʰ Hour)
(March to April) the Hedge
opens. Power depends
upon the Axle of a
Big Cart.

Hexagram 11: Tai -
Peace (3ʳᵈ to 5ᵗʰ Hour)
(February to March)
Heaven and Earth
Unite in the Image of
Peace. Thus, the Ruler
divides and completes
the Course of Heaven
and Earth.

Hexagram 19: Lin -
Approach (1ˢᵗ to 3ʳᵈ Hour)
(January to February)
The Earth above the
Lake: the Image of
Approach. Thus, the
Superior man is
inexhaustible in his will to
Teach, and without limits
in his Tolerance of the
People.

Hexagram 24: Fu -
Return (Turning Point)
(23ʳᵈ to 1ˢᵗ Hour)
(December to January)

Going out and coming in without error. Friends
come without blame. To and Fro goes the Way.
It furthers one to have somewhere to go.

Governor Channel (Yang)

Microcosmic Orbit

Fig. 3.2. The Governor Channel joins the energy centers of the back and
connects with the Functional Channel at the roof of the mouth to form the
Microcosmic Orbit.

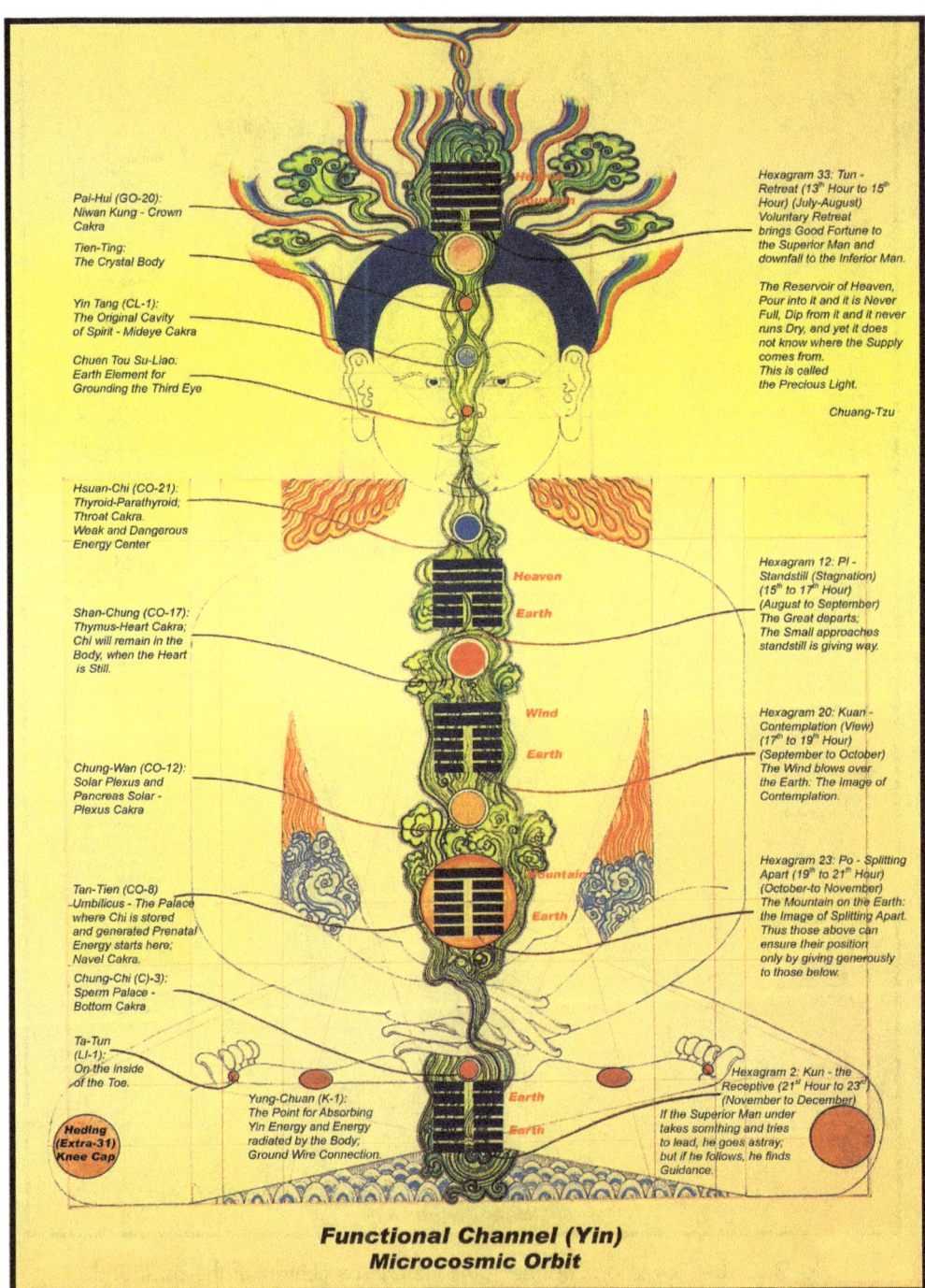

Pai-Hui (GO-20):
Niwan Kung - Crown
Cakra

Tien-Ting:
The Crystal Body

Yin Tang (CL-1):
The Original Cavity
of Spirit - Mideye Cakra

Chuen Tou Su-Liao:
Earth Element for
Grounding the Third Eye

Hsuan-Chi (CO-21):
Thyroid-Parathyroid;
Throat Cakra.
Weak and Dangerous
Energy Center

Shan-Chung (CO-17):
Thymus-Heart Cakra;
Chi will remain in the
Body, when the Heart
is Still.

Chung-Wan (CO-12):
Solar Plexus and
Pancreas Solar -
Plexus Cakra

Tan-Tien (CO-8)
Umbilicus - The Palace
where Chi is stored
and generated Prenatal
Energy starts here;
Navel Cakra.

Chung-Chi (C)-3):
Sperm Palace -
Bottom Cakra

Ta-Tun
(LI-1):
On the inside
of the Toe.

Heding
(Extra-31)
Knee Cap

Yung-Chuan (K-1):
The Point for Absorbing
Yin Energy and Energy
radiated by the Body;
Ground Wire Connection.

Hexagram 33: Tun -
Retreat (13th Hour to 15th
Hour) (July-August)
Voluntary Retreat
brings Good Fortune to
the Superior Man and
downfall to the Inferior Man.

The Reservoir of Heaven,
Pour into it and it is Never
Full, Dip from it and it never
runs Dry, and yet it does
not know where the Supply
comes from.
This is called
the Precious Light.

Chuang-Tzu

Hexagram 12: PI -
Standstill (Stagnation)
(15th to 17th Hour)
(August to September)
The Great departs;
The Small approaches
standstill is giving way.

Hexagram 20: Kuan -
Contemplation (View)
(17th to 19th Hour)
(September to October)
The Wind blows over
the Earth: The Image of
Contemplation.

Hexagram 23: Po - Splitting
Apart (19th to 21st Hour)
(October-to November)
The Mountain on the Earth:
the Image of Splitting Apart.
Thus those above can
ensure their position
only by giving generously
to those below.

Hexagram 2: Kun - the
Receptive (21st Hour to 23rd)
(November to December)
If the Superior Man under
takes somthing and tries
to lead, he goes astray;
but if he follows, he finds
Guidance.

Heaven
Earth

Wind
Earth

Mountain
Earth

Earth
Earth

Functional Channel (Yin)
Microcosmic Orbit

Fig. 3.3. The Functional Channel joins the energy centers of the front and
connects with the Governor Channel to complete the Microcosmic Orbit.

essence of life-force energy found in the organs, glands, and senses is transformed, purified, condensed, and combined with the universal force. The new form of energy that emerges through this process can effect positive changes in the human body.

During the Fusion practice, the negative emotions associated with each organ and each element are drawn out of the organs and transformed into a neutralized energy, thereby "balancing the weather" of the body's total energies. This neutralized energy can be blended with positive energies, also residing in the organs, and transformed into pure life-force energy. The Taoists have a saying: "Refined red sand turns into silver." This means that if you fuse all the different kinds of emotional energy together, they will adhere into a harmonious whole. However, unrefined, "unfused" energy will have the quality of sand, scattered about and unable to stick together.

The Pearl: Essence of Life-Force Energy

The pure life-force energy derived from the organs and fused together during the Fusion practice is crystallized into an energy ball. This energy ball can be perceived as a crystal or diamond, but is perceived most commonly as a radiant pearl. Forming the pearl is the first step toward transferring consciousness to a new realm.

Not all people perceive the pearl in the same way. Some might not see a pearl, but might recognize it as an acute feeling of awareness or as an intensified ability to concentrate. Some may feel a concentration of heat. All are experiencing the pearl as the essence of life-force energy.

This pearl is then circulated in the Microcosmic Orbit. While it is circulating, the pearl activates and absorbs the universal and earth forces. It also uses them to strengthen and purify the physical body, particularly the organs and organ meridians, glands, and senses. Later, the pearl plays a central role in developing and nourishing the soul body or energy body. It is developed further in the higher-level Kan and Li meditations.*

---

*For further details on the Fusion practices, including forming the pearl, see *Fusion of the Five Elements* (Rochester, Vt.: Destiny Books, 2007); for more information on the Kan and Li practices see *The Taoist Soul Body: Harnessing the Power of Kan and Li* (Rochester, Vt.: Destiny Books, 2007).

The Eight Forces

EIGHT TRIGRAMS SYMBOLIZE THE EIGHT FORCES

Each of the eight forces—Kan (water), Li (fire), Chen (thunder), Tui (lake), Kun (earth), Ken (mountain), Sun (wind), Chien (heaven)—takes form as a trigram formed of lines that are either yin or yang.

Kan—Water Yin / Yang / Yin

Kan is the power symbol of the element water, the gathering yin power, connected with the kidneys, ears, and sexual organs.

Li—Fire Yang / Yin / Yang

Li is the power symbol of fire, the prospering power, connected with the heart.

Chen—Thunder Yin / Yin / Yang

Chen is the power symbol of thunder and lightning. Chen is connected with the liver and the eyes, the wood element, and gathering power.

Tui—Lake
Yin
Yang
Yang

Tui is the power symbol of lake and rain, connected with the lungs and nose, the metal element, and contracting power.

Kun—Earth
Yin
Yin
Yin

Kun is the power symbol of earth, the stabilizing power of harmony. It is connected with the stomach and mouth, spleen and pancreas.

Ken—Mountain
Yang
Yin
Yin

Ken is the power symbol of mountain. It is a stable and strong energy, connected with the bladder, the right sexual organs, and the back of the skull.

Sun—Wind
Yang
Yang
Yin

Sun is the power symbol of wind. It is connected with the gallbladder and the base of the skull.

Chien—Heaven
Yang
Yang
Yang

Chien is the power symbol of heaven, the expanding yang energy. It connects with the left sexual organs, the large intestine, and the forehead bone.

THE FORCES OF NATURE AS THE EIGHT IMMORTALS

Beyond the visible, the eight forces of the universe are symbolized by the eight immortals (fig. 4.1 on page 26).

Representing the forces of nature, each of the eight immortals is associated with a particular geographical direction, season, color,

Fig. 4.1. The eight forces of the universe are symbolized by the eight immortals. In this arrangement of the trigrams the directions associated with each of the forces correspond to the usual compass-point directions found on any map, with north at the top and south at the bottom. We will follow this arrangement for our closer examination of each of the eight immortals.

planet, animal, organ, and so forth. Beginning with Han Hsien-Ku in the southeast, we will go around the pakua in a counterclockwise direction, describing the attributes of each of the eight immortals.

 SOUTHEAST: HAN HSIEN-KU

Han Hsien-Ku's Characteristics

Color: Purple (green)	**Direction:** Southeast
Force: Sun (wind) (+)	**Emotions (positive):** Kindness, forgiveness, graciousness, friendliness
Number: Four (4)	
Season: Late spring	
Energy: Great Yin (-)	**Emotions (negative):** Jealousy, anger, envy, rage
Period: 800 CE	
Planet: Pluto	**Chi:** Warming
Mental: Sensitivity	**Nourishes:** Tendon
Known as: Mountain Sage	**Animal:** Buffalo
System: Nervous	**Attitude:** Determination
Quality: Growing	**Teacher:** Lu Tung-Pin
Element: Air (wood)	**Organ:** Gallbladder
Movement: Generating	**Produces:** Tears
Symbol: Magic Flute	**Climate:** Damp
Gland: Adrenal	**Function:** Deciding
Seed: Sprouting	**Spirit:** Green Dragon
Tai Chi: Pull-down	**Sense:** Seeing (eyes)
I Ching: Penetration/following	**Sound:** Sh-h-h-h-h-h

Han Hsien-Ku (Han Xiang Zi) was born in the eighth century CE (see fig. 4.2 on page 28). He was a nephew of the great Tang poet and scholar Han Yu. He studied and prepared for the state civil exams, but—to the dismay of his uncle—he avoided taking them. He was an intelligent but wild child who disdained the pomp and vanity of the world.

Despite his expulsion from a Buddhist temple for rudeness and mischief, he delighted in stillness and obscurity. He was initiated into the secrets of Taoism by fellow Immortal Lu Tung-Pin while still a teenager, and quickly became absorbed in the practice of internal

韓湘子

Fig. 4.2. Han Hsien-Ku

alchemy. He probed the mysteries of heaven and mastered the five phases (elements) of energy. The sacred knot on his robe is a symbol of his success in combining the two energies of yin and yang into the one original energy.

One time Lu Tung-Pin carried him up to a vantage point on the mythical World Tree in order to show him the universe. Han Hsien-Ku fell from the tree and was killed but quickly resurrected himself. He was very poor, but totally unconcerned about it, for he was intoxicated with the love of the Tao. He performed wonderful feats and was able to foretell the future. He was able to make wine without grapes and flowers bloom in midwinter. One winter he magically grew a bunch of rose peonies and on each petal were verses written in gold that foretold the fate of his uncle.

He is often depicted with a bouquet of flowers. He carries a flute on which he plays the Six Healing Sounds. He is shown mounted on a buffalo, a mythical beast symbolizing the Taoist goddess Hsi Wang Mu, ruler of the west.

 EAST: CHUAN CHUNG-LI

Chuan Chung-Li Characteristics

Color: Light Green

Force: Chen (thunder) (+)

Number: Three (3)

Season: Early spring

Energy: Great Yang (-)

Period: 200 CE

Planet: Jupiter

Mental: Emotional

Known as: General

System: Tendons

Quality: Growth

Direction: East

Emotions (positive): Generosity, forgiveness, benevolence, benign

Emotions (negative): Blame, aggression, guilt, frustration

Chi: Moist

Nourishes: Nerves

Animal: Chimera

Attitude: Decisiveness

Teacher: Lao-tzu

鍾離權

Fig. 4.3. Chuan Chung-Li

Element: Wood (air)	**Organ:** Liver
Movement: Developing	**Produces:** Tears
Symbol: Feather fan	**Climate:** Warm
Gland: Hypothalamus	**Function:** Controls
Seed: Sprouting	**Spirit:** Green Dragon
Tai chi: Push	**Sense:** Seeing (eyes)
I Ching: Intuition/action	**Sound:** Sh-h-h-h-h-h

Chuan Chung-Li (Quan Zong Li) was born in the third century CE (fig. 4.3). During the Han Dynasty, he was an army general (Marshall of the Empire). After meeting an old man who taught him about the Tao, he left government service, and went to the mountains, becoming a wanderer and a beggar. Once while he was meditating, the stone wall of his mountain dwelling crumbled, exposing a jade box. The box contained secret meditation instructions on how to become an immortal. He followed the instructions, and one day his chamber was filled with rainbow clouds and celestial music. A crane arrived and carried him on its back into the regions of immortality.

After that he was able to wander among the heavens by himself. During a great famine he changed copper and pewter into gold and silver and gave it to the poor, thus saving thousands of lives. He taught Lu Tung-Pin the secrets of Taoism after convincing him of the emptiness of life, and persuaded him to join in his blissful life as a fellow immortal.

He is portrayed as bearded, and thinly clad. His hair is gathered in two coils on the sides of his head. His symbol is a fan, which he uses to revive and reincarnate the souls of the departed. Over 1,800 years old, he has often reappeared on Earth as a messenger of Heaven. He is mounted on a chimera, a mythical animal sacred to the Taoist goddess of immortality, Hsi Wang Mu.

 NORTHEAST: TSAO KUO-CHIU

Tsao Kuo-chiu Characteristics

Color: Blue (brown, associated with yellow and the center)

Emotions (positive): Fairness, openness, harmony, acceptance

Energy: Lesser Yang (-)

Period: 1100 CE

Planet: Uranus

Chi: Balancing

Nourishes: Flesh

Animal: Spirit Horse

Attitude: Stabilizing

Teacher: Lu Tung-Pin

Organ: Spleen

Produces: Saliva

Climate: Mild

Function: Balances-integrates

Spirit: Yellow Phoenix

Sense: Taste (mouth)

Sound: Who-o-o-o-o-o

Direction: Northeast

Force: Ken (mountain) (+)

Number: Eight (8)

Season: Early fall (Indian summer)

Emotions (negative): Worry, anxiety, false sympathy, distraction

Mental: Clarity

Known as: Mountain Hermit

System: Lymphatic

Quality: Equalize

Element: Earth

Movement: Centering

Symbol: Castanets

Gland: Pituitary

Seed: Ripen

Tai Chi: Shoulder strike

I Ching: Stopping/stillness

Tsao Kuo-Chiu (Cao Guo Jio) (fig. 4.4) is one of two royal brothers. Their sister was a Sung empress during the eleventh century CE. He was so ashamed of his brother, who was a murderer and a hedonist, that he gave away all his wealth to the poor and went into the mountains to seek the Tao. In the mountains he clothed his body with wild plants and lived as a hermit. After some time he harmonized his mind, body, and spirit until he could easily transform himself into the Tao.

Fig. 4.4. Tsao Kuo-Chiu

One day while roaming about his mountain realm he met two of the eight immortals, Chung-Li and Lu Tung-Pin. Lu Tung-Pin asked him, "What are you doing?" He replied, "I am nurturing the Tao and studying the Way." Asked where the Tao was, Kuo-Chiu pointed to Heaven. Asked where Heaven was, he pointed to his heart. Chuan Chung-Li beamed and said, "The heart is Heaven and Heaven is the Tao. You indeed found the truth and the way. You understand the origin of things." They invited him to travel about with other immortals.

His symbol is the castanets, which he plays in a soothing and relaxing rhythm to facilitate meditation and journeying throughout the universe. He is mounted upon a horse whose spirit may have helped him unveil the secrets of the Tao and immortality. He is said to be still living on earth.

 NORTH: CHANG KUO-LAO

Chang Kuo-Lao Characteristics

Color: Black (blue)

Force: Kan (water) (+)

Number: One (1)

Season: Winter

Emotions (negative): Fear, shock, stress, panic, doubt, anxiety

Chi: Chilling

Nourishes: Bones

Animal: Spirit Horse

Attitude: Willpower

Teacher: Lao-tzu

Organ: Kidneys

Direction: North

Emotions (positive): Gentleness, stillness, alertness, gratitude

Energy: Greater Yin (-)

Period: 800 CE

Planet: Mercury

Mental: Spontaneity

Known as: Mountain Hermit

System: Urinary

Quality: Absorbing

Element: Water

Movement: Gathering

Fig. 4.5. Chang Kuo-Lao

Produces: Urine

Climate: Cold

Function: Ambitions

Spirit: Blue Turtle

Sense: Hearing (ears)

Sound: Who-o-o-o-o-o

Symbol: Phoenix feather

Gland: Adrenal

Seed: Dormant

Tai Chi: Ward off

I Ching: Passion/danger

Chang Kuo-Lao (Zang Guo Lao) was born during the eighth century CE (fig. 4.5). He said that in a previous life he had been a grand minister to the legendary Emperor Yao (2357–2255 BCE). He was an old man and mountain hermit when he mastered the secrets of immortality and became "the Original Vapor." He had a fabulous horse that carried him thousands of miles in a few moments. Often he rode facing backward. Upon reaching his destination, he would collapse the horse, folding it like a piece of paper, and store it in his pocket. When ready to travel again he would take it out and moisten it with water to change it back into a horse.

Many of the Tang emperors invited him to court, but he usually declined to go. He entertained one emperor by making himself invisible and drinking poisons. The emperor bestowed upon him the title "Master of Understanding the Mystery," offered him a high position and his daughter in marriage. Chang Kuo-Lao declined both offers; when he then received an imperial summons, he lay down and died. He was buried in a coffin, but when his disciples opened it later, it was found to be empty. After this he was frequently seen alive.

His symbol is a tube containing wands or a "Phoenix feather" with which he can foretell fortunes and misfortunes. He is known to help souls to reincarnate. Even today in China, his image is found in the bedrooms of those who are trying to have children.

🌀 NORTHWEST: LAN TSAI-HO

Lan Tsai-Ho Characteristics

Color: Silver gray (gold)

Force: Chien (heaven) (+)

Number: Six (6)

Season: Late fall

Energy: Greatest Yang (-)

Period: 300 CE

Planet: Neptune

Mental: Intuition

Known as: Minstrel

System: Respiratory

Quality: Condensing

Element: Metal (ether)

Movement: Compressing

Symbol: Flower Basket

Gland: Thyroid

Seed: Falling

Tai Chi: Single whip

I Ching: Strength/creativity

Direction: Northwest

Emotions (positive): Righteousness, dignity, discipline, substantial

Emotions (negative): Depression, loss, gloom, dejection, down

Chi: Cooling

Nourishes: Skin

Animal: Elephant

Attitude: Vitality

Teacher: Lao-tzu

Organ: Colon

Produces: Mucus

Climate: Cool

Function: Stabilizes

Spirit: White Tiger

Sense: Smell (nose)

Sound: Sss-s-s-s-s-s

Lan Tsai-Ho (Lan Cai He) was born during the Tang Dynasty, and became the youngest male immortal at age sixteen (see fig. 4.6 on page 38). He was an entertainer who, like some ancient shamans, wore women's clothing and makeup. A street singer and a beggar, he gave away his money to the poor. Always dancing and singing, he walked about with one bare foot, followed by crowds who thought he was crazy. He wrote and sang songs that questioned this life, its delusive pleasures, and its ceaseless and unnecessary reincarnations. In winter he would sleep soundly in the snow with

藍采和

Fig. 4.6. Lan Tsai-Ho

steam rising from his body, a sure sign that he had mastered the techniques of internal alchemy. He was often found in taverns buying wine for everyone.

One evening, after singing and entertaining, he left a tavern and mounted a crane that had descended amid the sounds of a celestial chorus. The crane gracefully carried this "Holy Fool" off into the sky before an astounded crowd. His symbol is a basket of flowers, plants, and branches from trees associated with longevity, such as chrysanthemum, peach blossom, pine, and bamboo. He is mounted upon an elephant, a symbol of wisdom, strength, and prudence.

WEST: LU TUNG-PIN

Lu Tung-Pin Characteristics

Color: Metallic white	**Direction:** West
Force: Tui (lake) (+)	**Emotions (positive):** Courage, justice, appropriateness, boldness
Number: Seven (7)	
Season: Early Winter	
Energy: Lesser Yin (-)	**Emotions (negative):** Sadness, loss, dejection, sorrow
Period: 800 CE	
Planet: Venus	**Chi:** Drying
Mental: Intuition	**Nourishes:** Skin
Known as: Wise Sage	**Animal:** Tiger
System: Respiratory	**Attitude:** Vitality
Quality: Condensing	**Teacher:** Hsi Wang Wu
Element: Metal (ether)	**Organ:** Lungs
Movement: Contracting	**Produces:** Mucus
Symbol: Whisk sword	**Climate:** Dry
Gland: Pineal	**Function:** Strengthens
Seed: Falling	**Spirit:** White Tiger
Tai Chi: Roll back	**Sense:** Smell (nose)
I Ching: Joy/attraction	**Sound:** Sss-s-s-s-s-s

Fig. 4.7. Lu Tung-Pin

Lu Tung-Pin (Lu Dong Bin), sometimes called Ancestor Lu or Lu Yan, is the hero of marvelous wisdom who resides on Stork Peak (fig. 4.7). He was born during the eighth century CE and is said to still be alive. He was a Confucian scholar who converted to Taoism after being initiated into the secrets of internal alchemy by fellow immortal Chuan Chung-Li. He is mounted on a tiger, a symbol of the sacred energy that comes from the Taoist goddess Hsi Wang Mu, who rules the west. Lu Ting-Pin carries a horsehair whisk, which symbolizes his ability to fly through the air and walk on clouds. He is always portrayed with a double-edged ("demon slaying") magic sword strapped on his back. This sword of supernatural powers was given to him by a dragon. It allows him to hide in the heavens and to make himself invisible to evil spirits. His three-part beard symbolizes the three Thrusting Channels used in internal alchemy. He can travel thousands of miles in an instant and was known to roam about China seeking those with kind hearts, especially those who risked their comfort and well-being in order to help others in great need. Upon discovering such persons, he would use his supernatural powers to help them transform themselves into Taoist immortals.

He also took every opportunity to embarrass and punish the rich and powerful when he caught them oppressing those who were powerless and poor. The Chinese masses have always loved and respected this immortal, the "Ancestor Lu." He spent 400 years on Earth, and periodically reappears. He is accessible through mediums or through direct communication during meditation or shaman journeying.

 # SOUTHWEST: HO HSIEN-KU

Ho Hsien-Ku Characteristics

Color: Pink (yellow, which is associated with the center)	**Direction:** Southwest
	Force: Kun (earth) (+)
Emotions (positive): Openness, sympathy, assurance, certainty	**Number:** Two (2)
	Season: Late summer
	Energy: Greatest Yin (-)
Emotions (negative): Worry, anxiety, uneasiness, anguish	**Period:** 700 CE
	Planet: Saturn
Chi: Balancing	**Mental:** Mental
Nourishes: Muscles	**Animal:** Deer
Known as: Female Ascetic	**Attitude:** Stabilizing
System: Digestive	**Teacher:** Lu Tung-Pin
Quality: Neutralize	**Organ:** Pancreas
Element: Earth	**Produces:** Saliva
Movement: Centering	**Climate:** Mild
Symbol: Lotus blossom	**Function:** Balances
Gland: Parathyroid	**Spirit:** Yellow Phoenix
Seed: Ripen	**Sense:** Taste (mouth)
Tai Chi: Shoulder strike	**Sound:** Who-o-o-o-o-o
I Ching: Receptivity/docility	

Ho Hsien-Ku (He Xian Gu) was born in the seventh century CE, and she is still alive now, over 1,400 years old (fig. 4.8). She became an immortal at age fourteen after meeting fellow immortal Lu Tung-Pin, who taught her internal alchemy, giving her a precious rare peach of immortality. Soon after eating the peach, she was able to journey in her spirit body to pay homage to the great Taoist goddess of immortality, Hsi Wang Mu. The goddess delightedly carried her off to the gardens of boundless space, Ho Hsien-Ku's new home. She was able to cease her menstruation and conserve her life-force energy. She

何仙姑

Fig. 4.8. Ho Hsien-Ku

also gained the ability to nourish herself by feeding only upon sweet heavenly dew and the omnipresent chi. She spent her youth telling fortunes and flying and floating from mountain peak to mountain peak to collect herbs and food for her mother and the poor. She also frequently flew to the mountains to meet other female immortals.

She achieved great fame and was summoned to present herself to the empress of China. She ignored the royal command and instead ascended to Heaven in full daylight, disappearing from Earth. Some years later she was seen floating on a rainbow cloud above the temple of Ma Ku, a famous woman Taoist adept. Ho Hsien-Ku still appears to the virtuous, the innocent, and those oppressed people who are in great need of divine intervention.

She is shown holding a magic lotus blossom, the flower of openheartedness and divine brilliance, which symbolizes her power and purity. She is mounted upon a deer, a symbol of longevity and ceaseless energy.

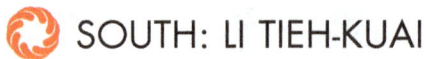 SOUTH: LI TIEH-KUAI

Li Tieh-Kuai Characteristics

Color: Red

Force: Li (fire) (+)

Number: Nine (9)

Season: Summer

Energy: Greater Yang (-)

Period: 200 CE

Planet: Mars

Chi: Heating

Nourishes: Blood vessels

Animal: Chimera

Attitude: Prosperity

Teacher: Hsi Wang Mu

Organ: Heart

Direction: South

Emotions (positive): Joy, love, respect, happiness, honor, patience

Emotions (negative): Hate, impatience, lust, arrogance, cruelty

Mental: Creativity

Known as: Lame Beggar

System: Vascular

Quality: Exciting

Element: Fire

Movement: Expanding

Fig. 4.9. Li Tieh-Kuai

Produces: Sweat

Climate: Hot

Function: Vitalizes

Spirit: Red Pheasant

Sense: Speech (tongue)

Sound: Haw-w-w-w-w-w

Symbol: Iron crutch

Gland: Thymus

Seed: Blooming

Tai Chi: Ward Off

I Ching: Attention/awareness

Li Tieh-Kuai (Li Tie Guai) or "Iron Crutch Li" (fig. 4.9) was born during the Han Dynasty (second century CE). He lived in the mountains for forty years, so devoted to practicing meditation that he often forgot to eat or sleep. Some legends say that the great Taoist sage Lao-tzu personally introduced him to the Taoist practices. Other stories say it was the Taoist goddess Hsi Wang Mu, ruler of the west, who taught him the art of immortality.

Depicted as a lame and ugly beggar, he was once a handsome and well-built man of commanding stature. His transformation occurred after his spirit body went to see Lao-tzu. He asked his student to watch over his physical body for seven days and prevent its destruction by keeping animals, insects, and other spirits from entering it. He told his student to burn his body after seven days if he had not returned by then. After only six days the student learned that his own mother was dying, so he burned Li's body and went to his mother's bedside. Li returned on the seventh day and wanted to enter his body. Seeing that his body had been destroyed, he entered the corpse of a lame beggar who had just died. He blew water on the beggar's bamboo staff and changed it into an iron crutch and a magic staff.

His symbols are the staff and gourd (a symbol of the universe). Having mastered the five phases of energy and successfully combining yin and yang into the one original energy, he is able to transmute matter with the staff and concoct medicines and potions from his gourd. He is credited with bringing his student's mother back to life using a magical potion mixed in the gourd. At night he makes himself very tiny and enters his sleeping quarters, which are also inside the gourd. He is well known to the poor, sick, and needy because of his reputation for benevolence.

He eventually ascended to Heaven in the form of a dragon, but frequently returns to Earth to help others. He is shown mounted on a chimera, a mythical guardian animal that symbolizes dignity and courage.

MEDITATING ON THE EIGHT FORCES

The pakua can be used in a meditation practice as a way to focus energy. The pakua creates a vortex that enables the practitioner to collect, gather, and condense chi. This vortex of energy can be used to not only create a strong connection within ourselves, but a harmonious relationship with all the forces of nature represented by the eight sides of the pakua. This is done by using the Fusion practice to gather and condense the abundant energy that surrounds us into something that is usable and digestible to the body.

The first step is to form four pakuas:

1. Front (or navel) pakua: Behind the navel, about one and a half inches inside.*
2. Back pakua: At the Door of Life, at the back of the body directly opposite the navel between Lumbar 2 and 3, and about one and a half inches in.
3. Left pakua: On the left side of the body, at the intersection of a mentally drawn line extending vertically downward from the left armpit, and a line extending horizontally to the left side from the level of the navel and the Door of Life. The pakua is about one and a half inches in from this intersection point.
4. Right pakua: On the right side of the body, at the intersection of a visualized vertical line drawn down from the right armpit, and

---

*The measurements pertain to an average-size body, but can vary for a smaller or larger person.

a horizontal line drawn from the level of the navel and the Door of Life, to about one and a half inches in.

Energy is brought into these pakuas, where it is then blended and transformed. Then, at the center of the body between the four pakuas, a self-center of being or control called the cauldron is created.

Location of the Cauldron: The Point of Control

The cauldron is located in the space between the navel and the Door of Life, but more toward the back of the body, in front of the kidneys. It is three inches in diameter. It is the place where all of the five elemental forces combine and transform into a very refined energy.

1. The energy from each of the four pakuas is balanced and condensed at its Tai Chi center, and these centers can glow with white or golden light.
2. The Tai Chi centers of the four pakuas spiral and blend this energy and direct it through the funnel-like backs of the pakuas into the cauldron. The center of the cauldron is usually at a point level with the Door of Life, although the center can vary with each person as much as an inch and a half up or down. In men who are top-heavy, the center can be lower. Women who are bottom-heavy can have a higher center. It seems that the thinner the person, the greater the chance the center point will be at the same level as the Door of Life and the navel. Once you have found it, you will readily know it is your center of awareness.
3. The front and back pakuas function as a pair in spiraling, drawing, refining, and condensing the energy into the cauldron.
4. The two side pakuas constitute a second pair to spiral, draw, refine, and condense the energy into the cauldron.
5. At the cauldron, energies are mixed further, blended, and condensed, and the pearl is formed (fig. 4.10).

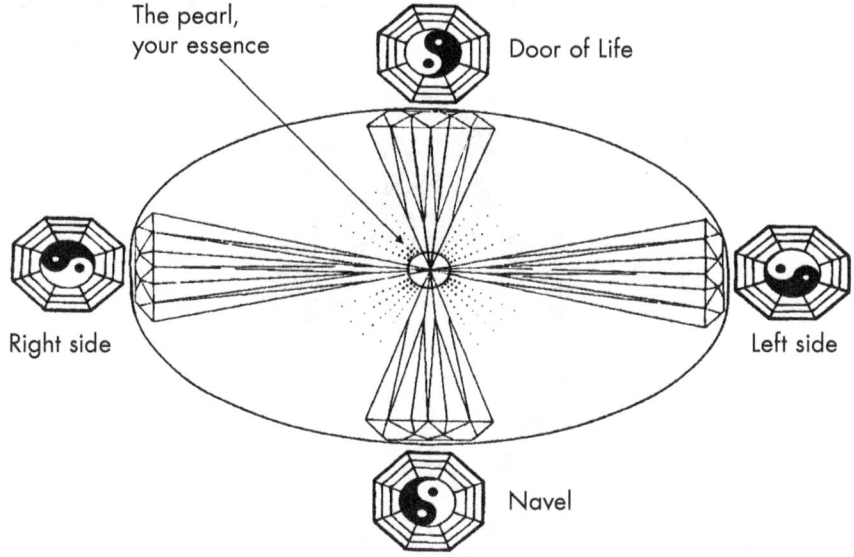

The pearl,
your essence

Door of Life

Right side

Left side

Navel

Fig. 4.10. The four pakuas condense energy into a pearl.

Once all these energies are condensed into a glowing ball of energy, the pearl is then circulated through the Microcosmic Orbit to open, heal, and revitalize the body, mind, and spirit. This is the beginning of the transference of consciousness to a new realm.*

The Six Healing Sounds associated with the immortals and linked with the organs are the foundation of another essential healing practice (see fig. 4.11 on page 50).†

---

*For complete instruction on the formation of the pakuas, the Fusion practices, and the Inner Alchemy of the eight forces, see *Cosmic Fusion* (Rochester, Vt.: Destiny Books, 2007) and *Fusion of the Five Elements* (Rochester, Vt.: Destiny Books, 2007).

†For further guidance regarding the Six Healing Sounds practice, please refer to *The Six Healing Sounds* (Rochester, Vt.: Destiny Books, 2007). For incorporating the Six Healing Sounds into the Fusion practices, see *Cosmic Fusion* noted above.

Six Cosmic Healing Sounds

Fig. 4.11. The Six Healing Sounds

The Twelve Animals

In ancient China, war and conquest, pestilence, flood, and famine displaced populations who carried their customs and beliefs from south to north and north to south, east to west and west to east, invading now, being invaded then, rulers today, refugees tomorrow, making enemies and forming alliances. One way or another the bloodlines mingled, and along with them superstitions, beliefs, and animal totems (see fig. 5.1 on page 52).

Nomads from west of the Huang and Yangtze Rivers settled near sources of water, the Huang valley and upper Yangtze. They cleared forests, planted crops, and raised sheep, cows, and horses, venerating the spirits of these creatures of nourishment. As local populations increased, so did their flocks and herds. Overgrazing eroded the pastures. When rain fell from the heavens washing away earth, the riverbeds became shallow with silt, and flooding destroyed land and livelihood.

Other spirits abounded. Tigers preyed on flocks and herds and were seen to have power. Snakes occupied the two extremes of the human spectrum: as phallic symbols through all ages and cultures they symbolized fertility, while their tendency to live in dark places such as graveyards connected them with death. Snakes also kept rats away and rats were seen as resilient survivors. Rabbit also stood for fertility and turtle for longevity, making a connection with the ancestors.

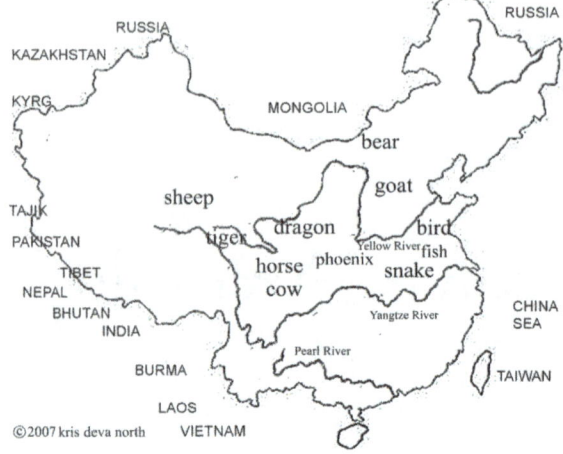

Fig. 5.1. The animal totems of prehistoric tribes in ancient China. The map shows modern surrounding states for geographical context.

As the snake people overcame other tribes, their totem absorbed the other totems. Snake swallowed bird and grew claws, swallowed cow and grew horns, and swallowed fish with scales and tail. Thus the elements of above, below, and within were united to form the Dragon, a creature with knowledge of the seasons, which slept through the winter and—when snow melted and plant life sprouted—rose from Earth to Heaven from where it hurled summer lightning and thunder. The Dragon's connection of Earth with Heaven led to its dominance as a symbol of divine power (fig 5.2).

Fig. 5.2. Dragon and Tiger, symbolizing fire and water, are two of the twelve animal totems of the Taoist medicine wheel and the Chinese astrological calendar.

BIRTH YEARS

Our birth year tells us our animal in the Taoist medicine wheel. In the Chinese calendar the year starts in February, so if you are a January child put yourself in the previous year. (Chinese New Year is based on the lunar calendar so does vary from year to year, but February 4 is a good median guide.)

In the table below, the years are color-coded in pairs according to their element: red is fire; yellow is earth; black (for white) is metal; blue is water; and green is wood. Yang and yin exist within each element: the first of each color pair is the yang year, the second the yin year.

BIRTH YEARS							
Rat	1936	1948	1960	1972	1984	1996	2008
Ox	1937	1949	1961	1973	1985	1997	2009
Tiger	1938	1950	1962	1974	1986	1998	2010
Rabbit	1939	1951	1963	1975	1987	1999	2011
Dragon	1940	1952	1964	1976	1988	2000	2012
Snake	1941	1953	1965	1977	1989	2001	2013
Horse	1942	1954	1966	1978	1990	2002	2014
Sheep	1943	1955	1967	1979	1991	2003	2015
Monkey	1944	1956	1968	1980	1992	2004	2016
Rooster	1945	1957	1969	1981	1993	2005	2017
Dog	1946	1958	1970	1982	1994	2006	2018
Pig	1947	1959	1971	1983	1995	2007	2019

In Chinese astrology the animal signs assigned by year represent what others perceive you as being or how you present yourself. There are also animal signs assigned by a person's birth month and the hour of the day in which a person was born. The tables below coordinate animal signs with the month and hour of birth. As in the table above, the associated elements are indicated by type color: red is fire; yellow is earth; black (for white) is metal; blue is water; and green is wood.

ANIMALS, BIRTH MONTHS, AND ELEMENTS

Rat	mid November to mid December
Ox	mid December to mid January
Tiger	mid January to mid February
Rabbit	mid February to mid March
Dragon	mid March to mid April
Snake	mid April to mid May
Horse	mid May to mid June
Sheep	mid June to mid July
Monkey	mid July to mid August
Rooster	mid August to mid September
Dog	mid September to mid October
Pig	mid October to mid November

ANIMALS, BIRTH HOURS, AND ELEMENTS

Rat	11 p.m. to 1 a.m.
Ox	1 a.m. to 3 a.m.
Tiger	3 a.m. to 5 a.m.
Rabbit	5 a.m. to 7 a.m.
Dragon	7 a.m. to 9 a.m.
Snake	9 a.m. to 11 a.m.
Horse	11 a.m. to 1 p.m.

Sheep	1 p.m. to 3 p.m.
Monkey	3 p.m. to 5 p.m.
Rooster	5 p.m. to 7 p.m.
Dog	7 p.m. to 9 p.m.
Pig	9 p.m. to 11 p.m.

In total, this makes for 8,640 possible combinations (60-year cycle [5 elements x 12 animals] x 12 months x 12 times of day) that a person might be. These are all considered in Chinese astrology.

LAYERS UPON LAYERS

Each animal is also associated with particular organ meridians of the body, each of which, as we have seen, has its time of peak energy flow, its "body-clock" or "organ-clock" time (see fig. 5.3 on page 56). The times of peak energy flow for each meridian correspond to the birth times associated with the animals of the zodiac. Each of these factors—meridian energy, element energy, animal energy—influence personality type.

Tiger—3 a.m. to 5 a.m.—Lung Meridian—Yin

Tiger people are sensitive, deep thinkers, generally sympathetic but can be short-tempered. Powerful and courageous, they get on with Horses, Dragons, and Dogs, not so well with Monkeys. Lung is responsible for jurisdiction in the land of the living.

Rabbit—5 a.m. to 7 a.m.—Large Intestine Meridian—Yang

Rabbit is a peacemaker, fond of gossip, tactful and kind. Rabbit people get along well with most others but especially with Sheep and Pig, perhaps not so well with Roosters. Large Intestine, Lung's partner, generates evolution and change, a Minister for the Environment, disposing of waste.

Dragon — 7 a.m. to 9 a.m. — Stomach — Yang

Every Chinese family, they say, wants a Dragon for a son-in-law. Dragons are lucky. They get on well with Monkey and Rat, not so well with Dog. Stomach sees what it wants, taking you forward to feast your eyes and fill your belly, and is the Official of the Granaries.

Snake — 9 a.m. to 11 a.m. — Spleen — Yin

Snakes are deep, full of silent wisdom. They help others and get on well with Rooster and Ox, less so with Pig. Spleen, the Treasurer, has the energy of nurturing resources, caring and sharing, in the nature of the earth element.

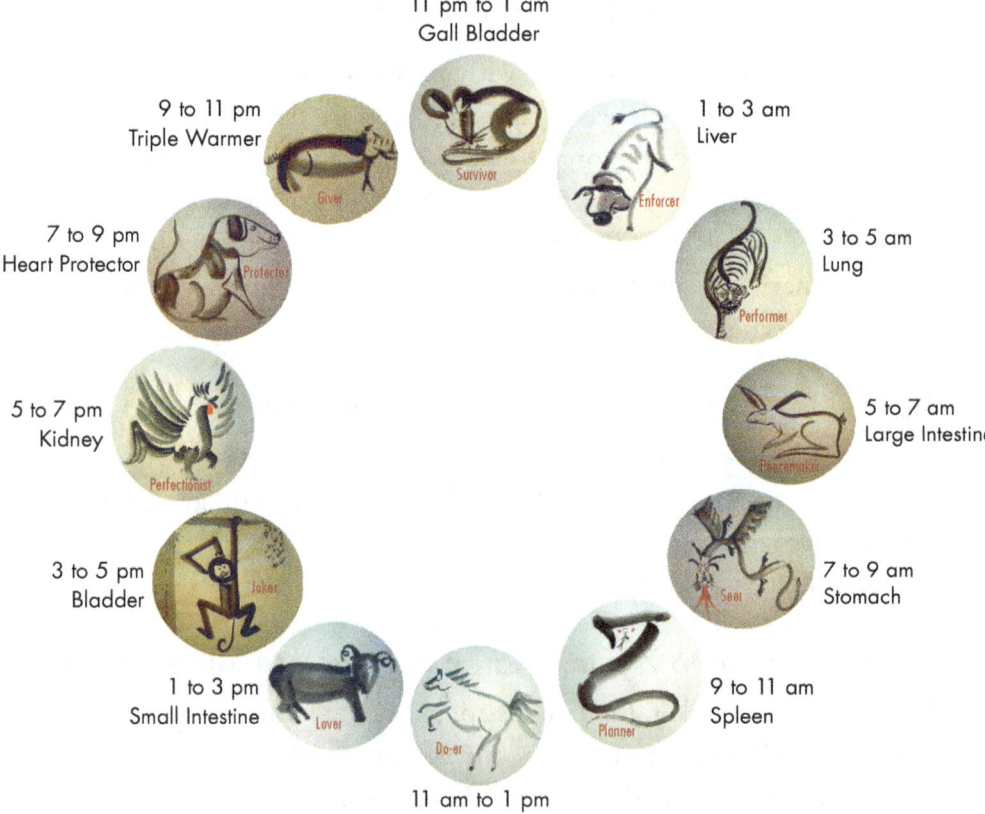

Fig. 5.3. Times and totems of the body clock

Horse—11 a.m. to 1 p.m.—Heart—Yin

Horse loves its freedom and defends itself by running away, until cornered. Horse likes Tiger and Dog, but has issues with Rat. Heart, a yin meridian, is the Sovereign, and carries spirit shining from the eyes. Its sensory organ is the tongue, the communicator.

Sheep—1 p.m. to 3 p.m.—Small Intestine—Yang

Sheep attracts love and generosity. Sheep gets on well with Pig and Rabbit but looks on Ox as a grazing rival. Close to the center of the Imperial Court, the Small Intestine is the official entrusted with creating change of the physical substance, the Minister for Recycling.

Monkey—3 p.m. to 5 p.m.—Bladder—Yang

Monkey is the erratic genius of the cycle, solving problems quickly before getting bored. Monkey is friends with Dragon and Rat but wary of Tiger. Bladder runs the length of the back, connecting with the past, routing through nerves along the spine related to the autonomic nervous system that looks after both action and relaxation.

Rooster—5 p.m. to 7 p.m.—Kidney—Yin

Rooster likes the world to know it's around and tells the world so. It tolerates Ox and Snake, has a secret admiration for Dragon, but has no time for Rabbit. Kidney, the guardian of ancestral chi, storehouse of genetic energy, excels through ability and cleverness, is entrusted with the reproductive essence, the spark passing from generation to generation as the moving chi between the kidneys. Kidney governs the bones, latticed crystalline structures sensitive to the transmission of etheric waves. In shamanic traditions of many first nations changing the bones is a step for transformation.

Dog—7 p.m. to 9 p.m.—Heart Protector—Yin

Dog is a loyal guardian who gets on well with Horse and Tiger but not Dragon. Heart Protector, a yin meridian, is Guardian of the

Heart and Minister of Fun, "who guides subjects in their joys and pleasures." Its time is the cocktail hour, and the time where in warm climes young people promenade looking for fun.

Pig—9 p.m. to 11 p.m.—Triple Heater—Yang

Feasting time. Pig is "giveaway," the manifestation of generosity. Pig is a sociable creature who likes everyone, especially Sheep and Rabbit, but is less keen on secretive Snake. Triple Heater, a prosaically mystical meridian, like the lotus, faces the sun, is rooted in water, and, unlike other meridians, has no individual organ association but distributes energy around the whole meridian network.

Rat—11 p.m. to 1 a.m.—Gall Bladder—Yang

Rats are survivors who work hard, acquire possessions, and are usually successful. Rat is friends with Monkey and Dragon but not with Horse. Gall Bladder, an "important and upright official who excels through decision and judgment," acts as Executive Officer to Liver and looks after lateral movement.

Ox—1 a.m. to 3 a.m.—Liver—Yin

Ox enforces the law, hates failure and opposition, gets on with Rooster and Snake but not with Sheep. Liver is competitive, the military General fighting to win. The energy of the element's season is springtime, of rising sap and urgent juices, the springtime of life that will not be denied. Competitive Liver energy extends into sport with its movement, focus, and desire to overcome.

6

The I Ching Hexagrams and Daily Life

With grateful thanks to Guillaume Bouteloup

The sixty-four hexagrams of the I Ching, the Book of Changes, form the outer circle of the Taoist Medicine Wheel. The Book of Changes explores the meaning of human affairs, based on the ideas that originated in the nomadic tribes that seeded both the Oriental and American cultures. Observing the pattern of relationship in the family and societies, business, government, and war, the ancient seers developed a guide to the way of change: the eight trigrams and the sixty-four hexagrams. Authorship is collectively attributed to Fu Hsi, King Wen, the Duke of Chou, and Confucius.

- Fu Hsi (3000 BCE) is said to have discovered the eight trigrams on the shell of a tortoise, which was widely used for centuries as an oracle, a farming, fishing, and hunting almanac.
- King Wen, founder of the Chou dynasty (1150–249 BCE), translated the images into words, developing the application of the oracle to the realms of commerce, politics, and social

relations. He wrote essays on the meaning of the sixty-four hexagrams while imprisoned by the Emperor Chou Hsin. When his son Wu overthrew Chou Hsin, King Wen took the throne. His son, now Duke of Chou, completed his father's work by writing commentaries on each of the six lines within the hexagrams.

- Confucius (551–479 BCE) added commentaries on the hexagrams and some of the individual lines in his work, *Ten Wings.*

As we have seen, each of the eight trigrams (composed of three parallel lines) represents one of the eight forces of the universe. Before the hexagrams were created the trigrams alone were used in early forms of divination. In this depiction of the pakua or medicine wheel—the Earlier Heaven Sequence, which is based on Fu Hsi's arrangement of the eight primary trigrams—they are represented in such a way that the polar opposites fall across from one another. Moving clockwise from the top, heaven is across from earth, wind from thunder, water from fire, and mountain from lake (fig. 6.1).

Pairing the eight trigrams led to the sixty-four hexagrams (8 × 8 = 64) (figs. 6.2 and 6.3). The coming together of the trigrams into the hexagrams represents the coming together of cosmic forces and human affairs, the mingling of Heaven (upper) and Earth (lower), subconscious and conscious.

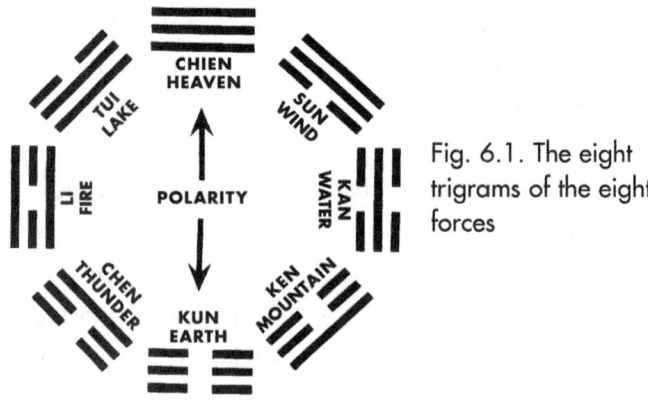

Fig. 6.1. The eight trigrams of the eight forces

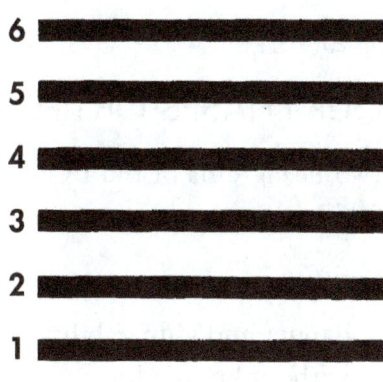

6 ▬▬▬▬▬▬▬

5 ▬▬▬▬▬▬▬

4 ▬▬▬▬▬▬▬

3 ▬▬▬▬▬▬▬

2 ▬▬▬▬▬▬▬

1 ▬▬▬▬▬▬▬

Fig. 6.2. Each hexagram of the I Ching is composed of two trigrams stacked one above of the other. The six lines of the hexagram are counted from the bottom to the top. Because the hexagram pictured here—hexagram number 1, Chien—is a doubling of the Chien trigram, we see six unbroken lines, the opposite of the Kun hexagram, number 2, which shows six broken lines. Most hexagrams, however, show a mixture of broken and unbroken lines.

HEXAGRAM CHART

Trigrams upper ▶ lower ▼	Chien ═══ Heaven	Ken ═ ═ Thunder	Kan ═ ═ Water	Chen ═ ═ Mountain	Kun ═ ═ Earth	Sun ═ ═ Wind	Li ═ ═ Fire	Tui ═ ═ Lake
Chien ═══ Heaven	1	34	5	26	11	9	14	43
Ken ═ ═ Thunder	25	51	3	27	24	42	21	17
Kan ═ ═ Water	6	40	29	4	7	59	64	47
Chen ═ ═ Mountain	33	62	39	52	15	53	56	31
Kun ═ ═ Earth	12	16	8	23	2	20	35	45
Sun ═ ═ Wind	44	32	48	18	46	57	50	28
Li ═ ═ Fire	13	55	63	22	36	37	30	49
Tui ═ ═ Lake	10	54	60	41	19	61	38	58

Fig. 6.3. The sixty-four hexagrams of the I Ching are formed from all the possible combinations of the eight trigrams.

GAINING INSIGHT INTO OUR PHASES OF LIFE

Each element is connected to one or two hexagrams of the I Ching, which correspond to the five phases of life.

Water

Hexagram 29, DANGER: A time of danger and vulnerability; the beginning of life's journey, without knowledge.

Wood

Hexagram 51, SHOCKING: Discovering, moving cautiously through the unknown.

Hexagram 57, PENETRATING INFLUENCE (THE GENTLE): Allowing influence, gaining insight and perspective.

Fire

Hexagram 30, SYNERGY (THE CLINGING): Aligning the elements to achieve together more than they could have achieved separately.

Earth

Hexagram 2, NATURAL RESPONSE (THE RECEPTIVE): Synthesis of learning, accomplishment, and confidence, leading to self-discovery.

Hexagram 52, MEDITATION (KEEPING STILL): Still mind, being in the moment.

Metal

Hexagram 1, CREATIVE POWER (THE CREATIVE):
Inspiration, energy, and will, in own space, accepted by others.

―――――――
―――――――
―――――――
―――――――
―――――――
―――――――

Hexagram 58, ENCOURAGING (JOY): Fulfillment.

――― ―――
―――――――
――― ―――
―――――――

PROBLEM-SOLVING WITH THE I CHING

In addition to providing insights based on the phases of life, the sixty-four hexagrams of the I Ching present different approaches to solving problems. Problems can, of course, be anticipated. To wait for a problem to arrive is like attempting a performance without any training. Imagine a ballet dancer going straight on stage without the hours of practice and rehearsal that makes her performance seem so graceful and effortless. Imagine a football team playing without practice, or a boxer entering the ring without being fit to fight.

How can we prepare for the vicissitudes of daily life, let alone "the slings and arrows of outrageous fortune"? Conflict, worry, or anxiety affect day-to-day life. Frustrations and doubts can block awareness, but the I Ching can help you to perceive the essence of the condition, suggesting present action, then showing possible outcomes of decisions. The I Ching doesn't give straight answers but allows reflection on what is the best course of action to take.

The Book of Changes is used to isolate the present moment by throwing three coins or dividing yarrow sticks with a particular question in mind. Divining the present situation offers a prognosis for the future. But it is not only about throwing coins and asking a question. The I Ching is based on your energy related to the cosmos; it is about your state of mind at the time of your consultation. If you study on a superficial level the answer will correspond: the I Ching reflects life. Regular practice assists in self-discovery. Modesty, honesty, ability to practice hard, and interest in learning lead to better comprehension of what the I Ching can do for you and your inner self. Within it runs the cycle of the seasons from conception to termination, how we live, what we feel, and what we discover along the way.

Sperm meets egg and the seed is planted. This energy comes from our parents. The fetus evolves in prenatal Heaven until birth, affected by all the energy around it, especially the mother's state of mind, feelings, and love. With birth begins life on Earth, the first breath, the start of our journey. A parent makes decisions; the child reacts. We are already in the yin and the yang. The first step is the freedom of going in the direction we want to go and the first word to say what we want to say. When we gain the ability pick things up, the choice is there already.

Consulting the I Ching

Your every action goes to the cosmos through connected energy and is sent back to you. Consulting the I Ching is an opportunity to discover yourself. Say you are stuck on something, finding no resolution. The first hexagram you receive by consulting the I Ching is a reflection of a blocked situation, one that doesn't allow you to move on. The reading will help you to realize that you are the only one who created that situation. Find out why you are doing this and why you have chosen this path. Every thing happens for a reason.

You can use any translation of the I Ching for the following exercise.

1. Sit back; think about the situation you created. What caused it? Formulate a specific question—not with a "yes" or "no" answer.
2. Next take three I Ching coins (these can be traditional Chinese coins with a hole in the middle, or three similar coins of any other type). Throw the coins on a flat surface, thinking of your question in a meditative way for each of six throws.

   Each throw will give you either a yin line (—— ——) or a yang line (————) derived from one of the following coin combinations:

> Two tails, one head is yin: —— ——
> Three tails is old yin (changing line): —— ——
> Two heads, one tail is yang: ————
> Three heads is old yang (changing line): ————

Your first three throws give you the lower of two trigrams, beginning with the bottom line and working upward. For example:

> Throw 3: —— ——
> Throw 2: ————
> Throw 1: —— ——

And the second three throws form the upper trigram, say:

> Throw 6: ————
> Throw 5: —— ——
> Throw 4: ————

Thus six throws yield a hexagram:

> 6. ————
> 5. —— ——
> 4. ————
> 3. —— ——
> 2. ————
> 1. —— ——

3. The hexagram you have built will correspond to a number. Using the chart given above in figure 6.3, you can determine the number (in the case of the example given here, the hexagram number is 64). Read the I Ching text on that hexagram to receive the part of your answer that comes from the cosmos. Understand and assimilate the answer before moving on.

4. Note the changing lines and the specific commentary related to them. All movement enters the hexagrams from below, ascends through the various states of change, and exits from the top. Thus the hexagram is read from the bottom line, the base; when the reading refers to specific line numbers, they should be counted from the bottom up.

5. The changing lines will create a second hexagram, which will be the continuity of the first one. The first hexagram is your present situation and the second one is what will happen in the future.

6. To go deeper in the answer, build a third hexagram with two nuclear trigrams. The lower trigram is composed of the second, third, and fourth lines of your second hexagram; the upper trigram is composed of the third, fourth, and fifth lines of the second hexagram. It is the core of the answer.

7. *Meditate upon this.*

Shamanic Practice

Magic is like religion. It can be of great benefit, or cause great harm. In Taoist magic as in the Tao, there is no judgment—we are all responsible for ourselves. As long as you do not harm another being, you are free to do what you want.

Few if any of the small rural communities that gave birth to Taoist shamanism remain, yet its relevance today as ancient secrets for modern living is undoubted. Communities change, times change. Shamanic practice must be relevant to the community it serves. Adapt or die is the law of extinction. As the dinosaur went its sorry way, so go those of the shamanic species who cannot adapt. While a shaman growing up in a specific tradition was bound to the form of that tradition, all traditions share the same substance. The shaman of the Tao follows the way of the Tao, the way of the Way. The eclectic practitioner follows his own way, her own Tao. Clinical studies, institutions, and Ph.D.s become the path of some. Others allow intuition, or "vision," to evolve practices, free of definition or limitation, relevant to their clientele or community.

We are fortunate to be able to include in this chapter guidance in the form of firsthand accounts from the realities of our practitioners in the Tao, those who serve to help others, seeking neither name nor reward. We are grateful for their consent to publish their stories while honoring their conditions of anonymity.

ROLE OF THE SHAMAN

When healing is needed, the body-healer is called to give acupuncture, massage, or herbs. If the sickness prevails, the shaman finds out from Spirit what healing is needed for the body to be whole again. Have we reneged on our "contract with Heaven," whereby everything is a gift and a blessing? Everything is love, and gratitude and thanks must be given even for hurt and pain. Then harmony can be restored between soul and body.

The shaman stands before the Tao and seeks answers:

- This healing has failed
- This body is ill
- What does spirit need to be satisfied and let wellness return?

These are the thoughts of intercession. Instead of presenting a solution in the manner of both conventional and complementary medicine, the shaman, having stated the situation, asks Spirit to "name its price," like a modern negotiator in a dispute between labor and management. Both sides want the same thing: satisfaction. The negotiator asks each, separately, what it would take to be satisfied. From this, he establishes common ground, shared satisfaction, from which to progress. The common ground may be small but, as negotiations develop, both sides realize that for either to get what it wants, something must be shared.

Spirit is no different. If Spirit wanted the death of the individual, Spirit would and could have caused it without further ado. That the individual is still alive means he has something Spirit wants. It is for the shaman to recognize this, to discover whether the individual can give it, or return to Spirit for further talks. Like the industrial negotiator, he must proceed from a position of power: acknowledgment of his role by both parties. Without that acknowledgment he is no more intercessor than supplicant, begging to be heard.

May it be assumed that Spirit acknowledges the shaman's role? If not, the shaman's task is to make Spirit understand, and this is where combat, trickery, bribery, and blackmail may become his tools. He may even disguise himself as Spirit and usurp Spirit's role to achieve the effect he wants.

We can't always assume that the patient acknowledges the shaman's role. Patients have been known to have their own agendas with illness. Thus the shaman might resort to costumes or actions to convince the patient that he has the power to heal, willy-nilly.

Transformation of self is the field of the shaman, from invisibility to overwhelming presence. Mediation with spirit needs as many tricks as a gypsy's pony. As war is the extension of politics by other means, so shamanic battle is the extension of negotiation. Journeys of subtle disguise into the enemy camp seek out the weapons of self-destruction in the patient's being.

Stepping Lightly in All Worlds

The understanding of power, the skill to see clearly, and the ability to step lightly in all worlds mark the shaman's practice. The external worlds above and below, the parallel realities of space and time, the internal worlds of her patients and her own, all are accessible to the shaman's journeying spirit. By acknowledging the patient's reality as a valid world for the patient, and the spirit world as valid for spirit, the shaman releases the constraints of physical healing systems. She has the power to bring a world within a patient or enable her patient to step into another world.

Being in the now, seeing in the now, open to all possibilities, ascendance of instinct over form, mark the shaman's thought. In particular, the power to help the patient see beyond his own world, the world that has induced his condition, to a new reality of personal health, for if the patient believes, then the preparation is done. "Whether you believe you can or you can't, you're right."

The Taoist's Hawaiian cousins call themselves Children of the Rainbow, and their shamans *kahuna*, who describe our thoughts as our reality. They tell us that we can change both our thoughts and our reality.

We embody every thought we have had, every thought another has had about us. We are the good we have done and the bad we have done, the good that has been done us and the bad done to us. The good and the bad of the past have become our thoughts. The good and bad of the present depend on how we react to events in the present. We can change the karma brought from before by our thoughts, and we can change the effect of what happens now, by our responses. We can choose, to live in the light . . . or the dark. Most of us live in twilight, with occasional patches of brilliance or shadow. Each thought is a choice.*

EXPANDING THE WORLD

What is your world, and where is it? For each of us in the center of our own unique universe, the world is what we perceive around us. We point to the moon and see the moon, but look at the pointing finger and the moon fades to obscurity. We look out the airplane window at lights twinkling far below. One of those lights is a house on fire. We cannot see that, nor hear the screams of those inside. They could see the lights of our aircraft if they were to look to the sky but there are more urgent things to attend to in their world.

The shaman has an interest in the worlds beyond her own, the worlds of others. She may leave her own world and step into that of another, or expand her own world to encompass that of another. Sometimes it is enough to see the world from another's point of view. Sometimes perhaps there is the need to hear or feel another's world, or to smell or taste it or sense it in other ways. Taking the basis of

---

*From Kris Deva North, "Calabash of Light," *Positive Health* 91 (August 2003).

shamanic practice as the healing beyond the physical, there must be ways to cross the borders of body. In Korea a shaman takes into herself the energy-body of her patient's diseased organ, heals it within her own world, and returns it to the patient.

Other worlds of other beings, worlds of spirit, the celestial realm, and the lower world all wait to be explored. Mapping the way to spirit shows how to get there but it is we who make the journey. The TV traveler sees, but the real-time seeker finds the experience. Many read books and believe they are having an experience and maybe they are, for it is only in the mind that we are truly free, to go where we will and do what we want, all in the comfort of our own control.

Travel to another world is going beyond our boundaries, stepping beyond our experience, releasing our need for safety, and embracing the unknown. How many have the courage for that? Or is courage necessary when surrendering?

How many of the plethora of institutions and individuals offering shamanic training offer a "risk assessment"? Instinct will throw us mindless into the canal to rescue a drowning man or under the wheels of a truck to save a straying child. In such instances limbic memory, in a flash of primeval assonance, assesses and discards the consequence to self of the likely outcome. This our soul does for us, but when an I solicits a You to train as a shaman, does the I assess the risk to You, or subconsciously cop out, or consciously rationalize with the creed of self-responsibility? At the end we stand before the Tao.

Journey of the Spirit

The shaman rides into the sky, the celestial realms of beyond, and down beneath the roots, and at human level, the conscious plane. Why are so many shamans "not of this world," not through anything they have or lack? Perhaps it is because they are ill prepared. Are we raised in the world of Spirit? Or in the mundane world where compliance and competition are the yin and yang of survival? Did we get good grades for expressing individuality, or for fitting in and being industrious? Was our spiritual training directed toward discovery of the essence of the Divine, or toward the form and ritual of hierarchical ceremony? Was our god the god of our own creation, or the God of our Fathers? From the depths of the Amazon to the panting heart of Rome, from the Dome of the Rock to the shrine of the Kaaba, we are taught to follow, to submit.

The shamanic neophyte undergoes shamanic death, a journey of spirit to release the programmed conditioning of the mundane. This begins in the course of the Kan and Li practice, when spirit is seeded, nourished, and grown from the cauldron, and returned to the cauldron to rest between journeys (see fig. 7.1 on page 74).* Those practices prepare the shaman to step through the inner eye, the first portal, to Heaven's Garden. That is the beginning of access to other worlds, and the ability to meet spirit guides and to help others heal. In all these practices, the pearl is always used to light the way and to transform self or others. Pearl is the focus, pearl is the essence, pearl is the key.

Time and Thought

In the world of the shaman all time is now, and when all time is now all space is one, and limitations of conditioned perception dissolve. In the early '90s I (Kris Deva North) spent some six months living alone on a mountain in south Thailand, meditating by day and occasionally making the journey down to the seashore. The following describes one of a number of extraordinary experiences I had at that time.

Walking along a sandy track by the beach, I suddenly found myself on the edge of a different reality. On my left, as before, the sea washing the sand, foaming gently in the song of the shore. On my right, where a moment ago had existed a coconut grove of well-spaced palms shading pools of grass from afternoon sun, now I saw a stone-age village. Nearby crouched a brown-skinned boy playing with sticks of wood. He looked

---

*For more information on the Kan and Li practices see *The Taoist Soul Body: Harnessing the Power of Kan and Li* (Rochester, Vt.: Destiny Books, 2007).

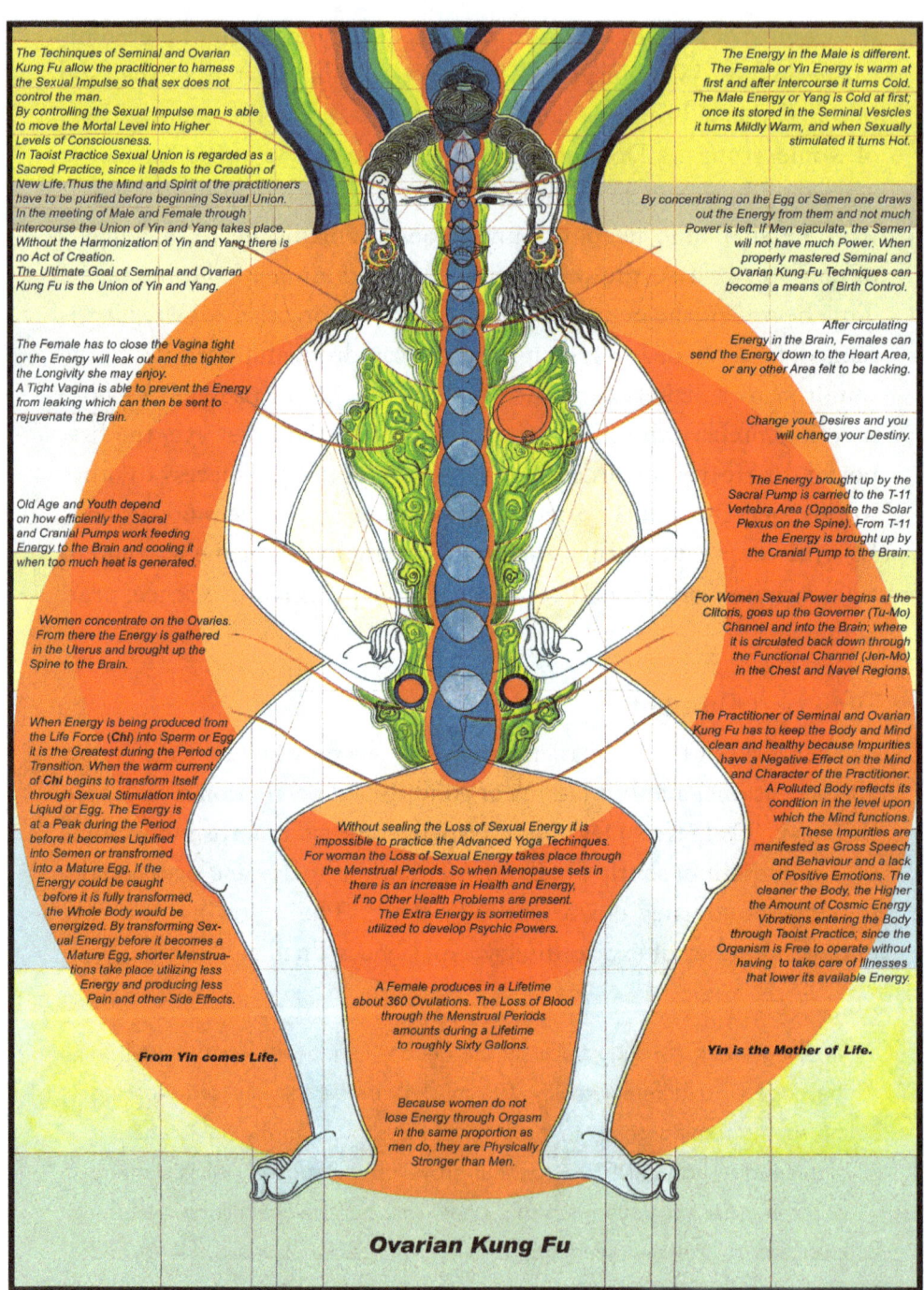

The Techinques of Seminal and Ovarian Kung Fu allow the practitioner to harness the Sexual Impulse so that sex does not control the man.
By controlling the Sexual Impulse man is able to move the Mortal Level into Higher Levels of Consciousness.
In Taoist Practice Sexual Union is regarded as a Sacred Practice, since it leads to the Creation of New Life. Thus the Mind and Spirit of the practitioners have to be purified before beginning Sexual Union. In the meeting of Male and Female through intercourse the Union of Yin and Yang takes place. Without the Harmonization of Yin and Yang there is no Act of Creation.
The Ultimate Goal of Seminal and Ovarian Kung Fu is the Union of Yin and Yang.

The Female has to close the Vagina tight or the Energy will leak out and the tighter the Longivity she may enjoy.
A Tight Vagina is able to prevent the Energy from leaking which can then be sent to rejuvenate the Brain.

Old Age and Youth depend on how efficiently the Sacral and Cranial Pumps work feeding Energy to the Brain and cooling it when too much heat is generated.

Women concentrate on the Ovaries. From there the Energy is gathered in the Uterus and brought up the Spine to the Brain.

When Energy is being produced from the Life Force (**Chi**) into Sperm or Egg it is the Greatest during the Period of Transition. When the warm current of **Chi** begins to transform itself through Sexual Stimulation into Liqiud or Egg. The Energy is at a Peak during the Period before it becomes Liquified into Semen or transfromed into a Mature Egg. If the Energy could be caught before it is fully transformed, the Whole Body would be energized. By transforming Sexual Stimulation before it becomes a Mature Egg, shorter Menstruations take place utilizing less Energy and producing less Pain and other Side Effects.

From Yin comes Life.

The Energy in the Male is different. The Female or Yin Energy is warm at first and after Intercourse it turns Cold. The Male Energy or Yang is Cold at first; once its stored in the Seminal Vesicles it turns Mildly Warm, and when Sexually stimulated it turns Hot.

By concentrating on the Egg or Semen one draws out the Energy from them and not much Power is left. If Men ejaculate, the Semen will not have much Power. When properly mastered Seminal and Ovarian Kung Fu Techniques can become a means of Birth Control.

After circulating Energy in the Brain, Females can send the Energy down to the Heart Area, or any other Area felt to be lacking.

Change your Desires and you will change your Destiny.

The Energy brought up by the Sacral Pump is carried to the T-11 Vertebra Area (Opposite the Solar Plexus on the Spine). From T-11 the Energy is brought up by the Cranial Pump to the Brain.

For Women Sexual Power begins at the Clitoris, goes up the Governer (Tu-Mo) Channel and into the Brain; where it is circulated back down through the Functional Channel (Jen-Mo) in the Chest and Navel Regions.

The Practitioner of Seminal and Ovarian Kung Fu has to keep the Body and Mind clean and healthy because Impurities have a Negative Effect on the Mind and Character of the Practitioner. A Polluted Body reflects its condition in the level upon which the Mind functions. These Impurities are manifested as Gross Speech and Behaviour and a lack of Positive Emotions. The cleaner the Body, the Higher the Amount of Cosmic Energy Vibrations entering the Body through Taoist Practice; since the Organism is Free to operate without having to take care of Illnesses that lower its available Energy.

Without sealing the Loss of Sexual Energy it is impossible to practice the Advanced Yoga Techinques. For woman the Loss of Sexual Energy takes place through the Menstrual Periods. So when Menopause sets in there is an increase in Health and Energy, if no Other Health Problems are present. The Extra Energy is sometimes utilized to develop Psychic Powers.

A Female produces in a Lifetime about 360 Ovulations. The Loss of Blood through the Menstrual Periods amounts during a Lifetime to roughly Sixty Gallons.

Yin is the Mother of Life.

Because women do not lose Energy through Orgasm in the same proportion as men do, they are Physically Stronger than Men.

Ovarian Kung Fu

Fig. 7.1. When yin and yang collide in nuclear
fusion at conception, spirit begins.

up and I saw he could not see me, suspended as I was between the two worlds, as if a shimmering transparent curtain hung between us. I knew I could step through the veil. Some yards beyond where he squatted on the hard ground, low lean-to shelters huddled in the lee of a rocky cliff. Other signs of life appeared: a sand-colored dog scampering around the feet of a woman who walked with a tall basket on her shoulder; two elderly men sitting on a stone, eyes lost in memories; slight movements in the shelters, signs of life and living.

I continued walking, slowly now. Should I step into that world or stay in my own? The beach scenery to my left changed as scenery does when you move through it, while the scene in the world to my right remained the same. For years I could not decide whether or not to step into the other world, for fear of what might happen, or what might not: that I might not be able to come back.

Once I had realized all time is now and all worlds one, and everything is perfect, I was able to make the decision. By then I had undergone shamanic death, changing of the bones in Nei Kung and dissolution of the physical in Kan and Li.* I had entered the void, becoming not part of the universe or one with the universe but myself becoming the universe. I had discovered the power of love that transcends all boundaries.

At first I could not get through the veil. It was like trying to get out of a clinging net. My physical body shook to free itself, and my upper part got through. I kicked the veil away from my legs and, taking one of the boy's sticks, pegged it to the ground so I had a marker to come back to.

The boy took my hand. He did not speak or smile. Nor did the old men, nor the woman with the basket but, nevertheless, I was at home and belonged there, and was not a stranger from another space-time. On my return to the previous "normal world" dimension I understood why none of this seemed strange. In that world communication was by thought and everyone knew what everyone else was thinking. Maybe thought, in our sense, is not the right description. It seemed more like the way animals in

---

*For more information on Nei Kung see *Bone Marrow Nei Kung* (Rochester, Vt.: Destiny Books, 2006).

a herd, or a flock of birds, or a shoal of fish, know what is what without "communicating" by any visual, auditory, or kinesthetic means.

The boy led me to a lean-to hut. Actually, he accompanied rather than led me because I knew where to go. I'm surprised now, even astonished, having come back, to realize that the woman in the hut is my partner in this world. There we had two children but here not yet! It was normal to see her, as if I had just returned from fishing. Again, no smiles, just a sense of normality, everything in place and a place for everything. Family and village life went on and I can only describe it from the perspective of this world I have come back to.

I met with other men in a cave in the cliff, to greet a returning hunting party. My mind filled with pictures of the hunt, men using shell-tipped spears and clubs, the death of two of the hunters, one of them my friend, a big animal falling, then being hacked apart with sharp-edged shells. One of us greeters had a pot of mixed colors pounded from roots. As hunters and greeters sat in a circle, he painted the story on the cave wall. The next group of hunters would be formed from those, including myself, who this time had stayed behind to look after the village.

It was simple to come back to my other world, this world where I am relating this account. In some way I was conscious of being myself as I am, without interfering with myself as I was in the stone-age village. When I lay down to sleep that night at the side of my partner there, I awoke at her side in this dimension. I know I can go back there at will and am looking forward to the hunt!

RITUALS AND PRACTICES

Rituals and practices are anchors, to take us away or bring us back, to give us a familiar reality to hold on to. While surrender lets go of the need for anchors and the goal is to wander free in all worlds, anchors such as setting the room right, clearing space, and self-protection help in the early practices. Later they can become obsessive or even addictive, such as the hallucinogens used in the Toltec and other traditions to preview where spirit can take you. Our early Fusion practices enable a person to seal the energy body against outside influence; more advanced practices (such as cutting and drilling) allow outside influence to pass through the energy-field without affecting us.* Through these different practices the Taoist comes first to a place where only intention is necessary, and ultimately beyond that, to where even intention can be left aside: no thought, no feeling, no learning, no teaching; no preparation except to be oneself. Perhaps this is the real short cut!

Enough guidance exists in the written world for an adept to select and develop his own form of ritual and practice, or to let it all go and enter the void.

SECRET KNOWLEDGE

In our New Age where anything goes, we can click a mouse for "secret knowledge" and see it offered on thirty-two million pages, with claims that this teacher knows more secrets than that one. How does one know how many secrets another knows? And if so, would they be secrets? With commerce the motivation, is not all suspect? Some follow a single path, some butterfly and never settle, some synthesize from different sources. Those who research, believing they discover secrets, discover only the secrets of others.

In the Taoist tradition secret knowledge is encoded in the classics, translated with wide and various interpretations, intrinsically corrupted by millennia of editing. For every statement can be found a contradiction. Where can we slake our thirst for the truth? Or do we follow the First Patriarch's admonition, to "Seek not the Truth, nor cherish Opinion"? Does doing things as they were always done mean they are correct, always and in everything? And does "correct" mean appropriate for individuals of different size, shape, culture, belief?

---

*For more information on the Fusion practices see *Fusion of the Five Elements* (Rochester, Vt.: Destiny Books, 2007) and for more information on the cutting and drilling practices see *Fusion of the Eight Psychic Channels* (Rochester, Vt.: Destiny Books, 2009).

Within each of us secret knowledge is stored in the DNA or in the vibrations of the soul. Opening to all possibilities allows knowledge to flow. Instinct rarely lies and inaccuracy is more likely a fault of perception. When the shaman is trained rather than chosen, the training provides a key to accessing secrets. By surrendering power to the teacher, the student puts him or herself in the hands of another, to be truly tested, to endure the experience of reality. Each of us who finds, evolves, or develops our own power knows the true secret.

The master acknowledges all traditions, the Tao all ways. When what would have been labeled as heresy in Christendom arises in the Tao, the master, honoring the freedom of thought that allows a different perspective, gives the heretic a blessing and a pinch of ash from the shrine to seed a new school. It is this innate tolerance and compassion that marks our Way.

INITIATION

Some say the modern human could not endure the initiations of old. Could the ancients endure the initiations of today?

The shaman is born. To be born he must die:

> *As sure is death for the born*
> *So sure is birth for the dead*
> *Like joy, like grief*
> *All things shall pass.*

Does the shaman recognize herself? Does the world, that is, her community, recognize her? Does she accept, acknowledge, reject, or ignore the burdensome gift? Many students seek a teacher for self-development, to attain a higher level, to enhance their power, or help others. Some are ticking boxes, others want to claim they have done such and such training with so and so. The shamanic teacher encourages each to find her own gift, helps each to recognize his limitations so he ceases to spend time, money, or energy in a fruitless pursuit; the teacher helps each to understand her own ego: the power of a strong ego that gives the resolution and fortitude to endure, and the weak that needs constant feeding. To reveal a shaman as yet unawakened, a teacher might set a task. A wise teacher agrees upon the task with the student, neutralizing excuses for failure. Eventually students leave to follow their own way, or another teacher. The moment of departure is the true initiation.

We are fortunate to have a firsthand account of a Tantric-shamanic ascetic of the Himalayas, a man without possessions of any kind. I (Kris Deva North) met this man living in a small Hindu shrine on the side of the road in Dharamsala.

I was a bus driver in New Delhi, twenty-seven years of age, and every day feeling I was in the wrong skin, that my skin didn't fit, not too large or too small, just didn't fit. I had a good job, regular money, enough food. But when I got this feeling I would imagine myself without a body, close to God. When I did this I felt . . . more than good. Beyond saying . . . so I told my parents I was going, and I went. I just sat down by the roadside and followed the first sadhu to come by. He was of the Seventh Order of Shiva. I followed him for seven years. He healed those who asked. Sometimes he would speak to me, teach me. In the seventh year he said to me, "go away." Now I am alone, at one with atman.

When asked if he felt rejected he answered, "What is rejection but a failure of expectation? For those seven years I had been learning to let go all that kind of self-indulgence." The simplicity of the man and his practice typify the soul shaman, he who knows himself beyond form or ceremony.

MEDITATION UPON DEATH

The shaman dies to be reborn. The mortal lets go of attachment to reality, to enter a state wherein he is no longer subject to the laws of the mundane world and its restrictions of time, space, and dependence on the senses. The Mau Mau (African-Kikuyu), Tantric (Indo-Tibetan), Taoist (Chinese), and other shamanic initiations across the world required violation of taboo. Form may vary, but substance is the same. We are fortunate to have the firsthand account of a modern initiate who participated in a Universal Healing Tao workshop in Devon, England.

Journey to Death and Beyond

They had warned us it would be hard. For days they alluded to our last day and on that day, they woke us before dawn. Huddled in blankets, we gathered on grass crisp with cold.

"Prepare for your last journey. Savor each moment of your time on earth, the mundane dimension you have become used to all the years of your life."

We began to walk, watching our breath clouds in the dark, feeling the grass crunch, then a stony path.

"Feel the ground beneath your feet, the earth that has supported you, provided you with all your needs."

We passed between high hedges, dark, green, full of shapes. The sky lightened.

"See the colors of the world, the shapes, the movements of the wind."

An owl screeched as we left the woodland. The moor waited, vast, open and silent. A rabbit lay dead on the road. The shaman picked it up. Had he placed it there? He passed it round the group. Some took it quickly and handed it on at once. Some inspected it from all angles. A few held it and stroked the still-warm little body. How had it died? There was no sign.

He laid it on a stone and led us between fields of bracken. Sheep marched ahead, white woolly bobbles in formation, ignoring everything as they headed to some meaningless destination. I felt like that, marching in the center, as the group spread out over the moor. Wild ponies grazed, white on green, looking without curiosity as we passed.

We came to a stone circle and entered from the east, turned to face the sunrise, red sky in the morning, and followed the shaman through the ritual greeting. The air warmed. Without warning he removed his clothes and signed for us to follow. Unsuited, we stood naked on the moor, a circle of souls ready to fly.

"Farewell to desire and aversion," he cried and fell to the earth, rolling among sheep-droppings and horse dung. We stood, shocked. Was this really a part of it? And yet, it must be, I found myself thinking. To be a different person I must do different things and I knew from the years of trying by myself that I had always been careful to choose to do what I could either do easily, or found impossible. In the submission of ego I had submitted to the shaman. I could not tell the thoughts in the minds of my colleagues. We had been told the process was of self-selection, that each of us would find our own glass ceiling. For some the glass ceiling arrived this early morning, on this first test of rolling naked on damp grass over piles of shit.

The decliners were led away by the shamanic acolytes. They had been through this initiation in years before, got through everything and would stay on this path until finding their own limits. For a moment I envied the departed. We knew their fate, having been offered this opportunity at every challenge in the days leading up to this. They would be taken down to the manor, to hot showers and warm clothes, to hearty breakfast, and then return to the mundane dimension where doubtless they would spend their future rationalizing, some claiming to have trained under the shaman, others denying him and offering their own easier version of access to the Divine.

Grass-rash itched my skin, except where lumps of turd stuck. We were still many, two dozen of us wondering what would happen next, when the shaman picked up a piece of shit, popped it into his mouth, chewed and swallowed. More departures, heading for a less tasteful breakfast. Would I tell my grandchildren I had eaten poo for my spiritual development? It was not as bad as I had anticipated, in that fleeting moment as you are about to do something that had never even crossed your mind.

We ran naked through waist-high bracken regardless of what was underfoot and came out breathless and high-spirited.

"Savor the moment!" he called. Did we believe we were about to die?

At one level I was convinced my life as I knew it was about to end. At another, the cynical gremlin muttered "bollocks, bollocks, bullshit, and bollocks." The shaman lined us up.

"This is the last time I shall tell you," he began, "it's only make-believe. You are not really going to die. Whatever we say or do to you, whatever you feel or hear, see or smell, in three days time you will be back on a train to the mundane. There will be moments," he looked at us from under his brows, warning, "moments when you will be afraid."

Beside me, Tun Lo sniffed his contempt. I found myself wondering why he was here, this small man who had started so much and completed so little.

"Embrace these moments. Taste the fear: let it fill your senses. If it gets too much, give yourself a pinch and tell yourself—they're just having a rant, none of this is real." He paused. "Unless you believe it."

I heard Ni Ling sob. She would enter the moment and boast of it for years, unlike her friend Yu Tan who would look into the eyes of the Goddess and flee.

We walked in silence back toward the manor. My head reviewed the night before. We had been told, "This is it," and after dinner led hooded over rough ground toward the sound of drumming. Blindfolds off, we danced around a mighty fire, sang songs, and celebrated being alive. We painted each other's bodies with signs and symbols, made circles of light with sticks of fire, and crawled through the narrow entrance into the sweat lodge. We sweated around hot stones, said prayers and dedications for the healing of self and others, and after some hours emerged, sweated out, dry skin chilly in the night air. A few stars lingered before slipping behind clouds.

The fire had become a carpet of burning red and the shaman walked across it. The acolytes followed, strolling at leisure except for Heavy Han who danced a circle on the glowing coals.

We initiates were expected to follow. Thunder hit my heart and my mouth dried to leather. They told us to imagine we were walking on cool moss. Most of us crossed the fire that night. The few who didn't left, and there were some surprises—it seemed the bigger the mouth the weaker the will. I was elated. I did the fire-walk! It had felt warm, not hot, but Ah Lee and Mimoy were burnt. More surprises.

Afterward we had been fed rice pudding! And left to sleep on the floor "before being measured for coffins" jested one of our "Angel Guides."

In a silence deeper than just not talking we got back to the manor. A feast had been prepared, "the Last Supper," with mystic chanting in the background. The menu on the blackboard read "Death by Chocolate for dessert. Ha Ha."

After the meal we cleared tables, then sat and waited, watched over by the Angels. But they were different. All the days and hours before they had been kind, helpful, smiling, encouraging us in our first steps into this new world. Most of us had experience of one or another esoteric path so the concept of trust and belief was not unfamiliar. Our group was typical of New-Age seekers. There were those who came from management or professional backgrounds, attracted perhaps by the idea of doing something completely different. Jim Bo was a corporate lawyer, Ka Tee a management consultant, Wee Lee a top PR guru who had dined with celebrities—a feat to remember? Ha Lee had lunched with royalty and shaken hands with the Dalai Lama.

Now we sat, quiet, submissive at the tables and the Angels were not smiling. Two wore masks, from comical to terrifying, two their own faces as if turned to stone. We "mortals" each with our own thoughts wondered what was next. They had told us modern man could not endure ancient initiations. I wondered if ancient man could endure the fakery and foolery of the New Age. In days of yore he was condemned to life in his village, a life of order, regulated and restricted by custom, or to leave and wander among strangers. Nowadays we are free, free to go where we will, learn anything from anywhere, to go crazy in our own thoroughly modern way.

"Hello. I'm Death." The shaman had appeared, seated at the high table, his manner friendly, conversational. "You seventeen have survived the ordeals of the past few days and hours. Now it's over. You're going to die but, let me assure you, you are in safe hands." He smiled and held up his hands, palms toward us. I noticed the curved knife like a huge paperweight on the table in front of him.

"I'll just run through my qualifications for the job," he went on. "I have handed out death in this life and lives before. My spiritual ancestry involved the killing of many. Now I am back, taking the chance to clean my karma, to help you on your journey of death to this life."

He picked up the knife. Its curved blade flashed. He made a cut in the back of his hand. Blood dripped on to the table. "My tradition," his face was impassive, "is that now she has drawn blood, she cannot sleep again until she has slaked her thirst."

The room was electric. This sudden shock of reality had us frozen in our seats. I heard a chair scrape the floor behind me.

"No," he said, "now you have come this far you cannot go back." A rush of Angels held down whoever it was who had tried to move. "You have seen and heard too much." He shuffled papers, glanced down at them, and looked up at us again.

"Who has made a will?"

I held up my hand, remembering Varanasi, standing among the funeral pyres, smelling death, hearing the crackling of wood, the popping of skulls, feeling the heat, seeing the crisping of skin and the melting of bone. When I returned home, I had drawn up my will and paid for my funeral.

"So. Less than half. And you others, what were you thinking, when you elected to undergo a death? That it was a game? Well, suppose it wasn't. Suppose you were really about to die. Suppose, in fact, that you had died on your way here, circumstances beyond your control, a traffic accident, plane crash, whatever. What kind of mess would you be leaving behind you?"

I could feel the minds of those around me. They had never thought of this. And nor had I until I stood among the burning dead and understood the fragility of the veil between us.

"And who would be cleaning up your mess for you?"

He spared us nothing.

"Did you say good-bye to your loved ones? Did you tell them you loved them?"

Silence, the silence of fear, the silence of guilt, and a few sobs of regret.

The shaman grinned. "Relax. You will have the chance to do all those things." He handed the papers to the nearest Angel, a tall one wearing a death's-head mask in front and a clown's face behind, who gave us each one.

It was a will. I read the words to the background of his voice telling us how privileged we were to have the choosing of our time to die, to have the choice even of the method, "bearing in mind," he said, "that it must be within the resources available to us here and now. To choose to die peacefully of old age here and now is as unrealistic as to choose a terminal illness."

The will-paper had boxes to tick—slashing, burning, poison, stabbing, drowning—would they hold our heads under water in the pleasure-pool of the jacuzzi? And the choice of how our remains should be disposed of: burning or burial, being eaten, dissolved in acid, or left out with the trash. The will form ranged from outrageous to comical to poignant—what would be your last words, how would you say good-bye to your loved ones, what in life would you do different if you had the chance . . . and at the very end, the question: how would you answer if all this were real?

They collected our wills, witnessed by Angels, and then we sat, under guard. One by one we were taken out, an Angel-demon holding each arm, and marched toward a din of hellish music. Now I was beginning to feel scared, but in a way ready to be tested. The room I left behind was full of sobs and snuffles as people with less self-discipline let their fear flow. As I approached the Gates of Hell they flew open and Yu Tan ran out, eyes staring, face distorted in horror. "I'm leaving," she screamed, "I'm going. I'm not going to die, I'm not, I'm not."

They let her go. They had observed her weakness over the days before, behind the screen of seeming strength. She had broken her addiction to drugs three years ago but still retained only a slender grasp on reality and suffered from delusions. Later she told me that when she looked into the eyes of the Goddess she felt she was losing herself.

The Gates closed behind me. A depth of darkness led to a shrine. They forced me to my knees and gave me a candle to light and place among others, saying that when its flame expired then so would mine. The shaman knelt to my left. He indicated I should look up. There she was, terrifier of the ignorant and protector of the enlightened. I looked into her eyes. My heart slowed, my breath calmed, and I felt a sense of peace fill my soul. Then I was jerked to my feet, dragged by the arms and flung to the floor. They laid me out like a corpse, hands folded across my chest like I had seen the effigies of medieval knights on cathedral tombs.

I focused on my death but was aware of other bodies being dragged and dropped, and all the while the hideous music sounded the screams of hell and belching demons.

Sudden silence. I could not help but open my eyes a sliver, and saw shadows of the acolytes. They moved among the bodies. I squeezed my eyelids shut again, to concentrate on being dead but too much sound of movement kept me aware of being alive. Then a whisper beside me, followed by the unmistakable whine of little Tun Lo. "I don't want to get up. I'm perfectly comfortable here, thank you," then, "No, I'm not going to move. I'm very happy as I am." What was going on?

A shadow loomed over me; a hand alighted on my arm. The voice of the Red Angel whispered, "Get up." I did so and she bound my eyes with a cloth and helped me to my feet. Was this it? To be taken out for execution? Till now, the death meditation had been all in my mind after the encounter with the Goddess, preparation of the will and the last meal. Was it to be more than a meditation? I had prepared myself and was determined to act my part to the full, or to be as passive as death deemed right.

I trod a stone cold floor. Someone else had joined the Red Angel, I could not tell who, and they led me through doors and over different floors to somewhere in the manor I had not been before. I tried to keep a sense of direction until realizing it was an old trick of my survival training, not appropriate now.

We came to a halt, the blindfold was taken from my face and before me sat the shaman on a plain wooden chair. My impression of the room was of blank walls and feeling cold. Two Angels stood either side of him, the Red Angel bare breasted, face covered by a furry cat-mask, and the tall figure in the death's-head-clown mask, holding an axe. I braced myself. How far would they go?

"If you were given another half-hour of life, what would you do with it?"

Startled, my mind raced through the possibilities. I had no partner to comfort me in my last moments on earth. My path had been solitary for several years. I had no great desires to fulfill before I died. My last wish sounded quite mundane. "I guess I'd spend it on the beach, in the sun," I ventured.

The shaman's response was sharp, although the voice was kind. "And which beach would that be? And how would you propose to get there and back here in half an hour? Are you taking this seriously? You have been offered another thirty minutes of life in this world, in this reality of here and now, and you are asking for a fantasy."

I was mortified. My ego cringed as I realized how all these days I had considered myself more dedicated, more into the meditations than others, superior. Now I had shown myself up as the shallow fool I had always known myself to be. The moment of truth weighed upon my spirit.

"I'm sorry. I don't care what I do with the last half hour. I'll spend it any way you say," was my next attempt at being in the moment, free of attachment to desire or aversion. But they would not collude.

"So. You want someone else to take responsibility for your last moments on Earth?"

I was a fish on a hook and they would not let me off. I had really to think about the reality of what I would do with another thirty minutes of precious life, in the circumstances in which I found—had placed—myself, in what I thought was a path of spirit. What did I really want? I thought of what being alive meant to me, and the answer was suddenly easy.

"If I were given an extra half-hour before I die, I would spend it walking in the trees, dancing on the grass, feeling the wind or the rain on my skin, lifting my face to the sky, digging my toes in the earth, just being in nature."

"Granted," said the shaman, "take him out."

Is this a trick?

○

Others were outside. The sun shone pale but warm and the grass felt good. I strolled the grounds of the manor. My friends, cohorts, and colleagues, sarong splashes of color on the lawns and in the woods, fulfilled the last wishes of their extra half-hours. Some ran about naked; others quietly meditated in nooks and crannies. I saw Monkey disappear into a bush hand in hand with two giggling women. Cries of pleasure rose from the ornamental island in the pond, where beneath the oak Juanita straddled Bruno, riding him to climax. Three men watched from the grassy bank opposite. Elsewhere I found Leo in solo cultivation, leaning against the trunk of an elm, legs straight out, eyes closed, hand a blur. Five girls danced a circle on a terrace, singing songs of the Goddess.

Crow flew overhead, and I went to sit in stippled shade under the ash. I caught myself thinking uncharitable thoughts of Tun Lo being "perfectly comfortable" where he was, missing out on some real enlightenment. Why, even on the brink of death my judgments abounded! I closed my eyes and turned my thoughts inward.

A distant bell summoned us to the upper terrace. The acolytes had us sit in a circle. Unmasked, in the sarongs we had all worn throughout the retreat, they looked normal and friendly again. The shaman joined us, smiling.

"A last ritual," he said. "Consider, now, what would be your epitaph?"

What would I say about myself? I was not sure. What words could summarize my life? When my turn came I said "Not sure" and everyone laughed. I hear others declare theirs, from pompous to sincere, some using quotations, others struggling with simple words.

Then we had to say good-bye to each other, to look into each other's eyes and speak what we truly felt. This was hard. I observed in myself that I tended to hold others in contempt. I then and there resolved to change, right now! I could see their good as easily as their failings. Flashes of my childhood brought memories of uncles telling me I was so lazy I wouldn't be bothered to breathe if it didn't come naturally, instilling negative motivation, polarity response. Here, now, people were looking into my eyes and saying wonderful things to me. "I think you're wonderful too," I'd respond.

It was a strange time. We went from choked up with emotion to smiling delight, hugging each other tight in what we now believed were our last moments together.

They lined us up at the Gates of Hell, morphed into a wooden door decorated with a pakua. An acolyte briefed us. "When you're dead you must lie still, but when it becomes too painful to stay in the same position, you can shift. Pain tells you that you are alive, and becomes a distraction. If you need help or have to go to the toilet, sit up. An Angel will come and guide you. Keep your blindfold on all the time. When the bell rings, sit up. When the gong sounds, lie down."

"How long will we be dead?" asked someone. The Angel stared at her. "Forever, stupid," came from down the line. Nervous laughter. Apprehension sat heavy as we filed back into the Death Chamber, to our deathbed mats. Acolytes prowled the spaces between. Tun Lo lay curled up asleep in his perfectly comfortable place. Candles flickered around the shrine at the end. There were no visible windows or doors. The walls rose into darkness.

"Put on your blindfolds now, and sleep," said the Angel, "and wake at the first bell. You will be guided to your death. Remember, this is a sealed chamber. The thoughts you think in here will not go beyond these walls. Nobody in the mundane dimension will be affected by your thoughts here. This chamber of death is sealed from the world."

The gong sounded. I lay down, wondering what he could mean.

It had been late afternoon when we came in. Not sleepy, I fell into a dreamy trance. Anxiety had gone, replaced by a strange peace. I had done all I needed to do to depart this life in good order. Time passed. I dreamed of nature, then an old movie, something green with an old man dying to the sound of the four seasons. Would it be cosmic soup awaiting, or any kind revelation of life before or after, or the vision of God instilled with the catechism of my childhood? I had never understood the concept of perfect happiness from just gazing at God. In latter years I had contemplated the nature of god-ness. Once, roaming down Victoria Street to the McDonalds in the churchyard of Westminster Cathedral, accosted by zealots with "Do you believe in God?" I had answered, "What, exactly, do you mean by God?" They seemed flummoxed. "Why, God. You know, God! In the Bible," as if it were a neighbor I saw every day, or a famous brand. "What is your understanding of God?" I asked, and waited, somehow envying their blinkered commitment to what they knew not. My patience ran out and I went to meet my children.

They would remember me, of course. Who else? Friends, colleagues, wives, lovers. It was time to make peace, rolling out my map of life, the good I had done and the bad, and I dreamed of going back to each situation. The bell rang and a voice intruded, guiding us through a last ritual of Kan and Li, through the inner eye and down rainbow steps into Heaven's Garden.*

"Your last night on Earth, your last night with your beloved." Chinese Tea Ballads, love songs of Abba and Lennon-McCartney, and the tones of the shaman filled the air. "Gaze into the eyes of your beloved and see the love, feel the love, the desire, and see it reflected in the eyes of your beloved.

"Hear the sounds of passion, the breath of your lover on your face.

"Feel the touch of your beloved, stroke your hands, let them stray, caressing, enticing, arousing . . ."

I let myself go in the surround-sounds of ecstasy and felt the release all around me. Why hold back tonight? The Upward Draw† was designed to retain the essence of life and here we were crossing the threshold of death.

After the storm, the gong. All quiet, but for the breathing of humans after lust. Sleep came then, deep and dreamless as I drifted away to the words of the Lama, on the moments of perfection, when we want for nothing, the moment of climax, the moment of sleep, the moment of death.

Had I known what would happen next I might never have enrolled myself in this initiation but then I imagine that none of us would have. But it made me angry before I realized, understood, and valued the benefit of the next event.

"And now, call in your loved ones, those closest to you in the life you are about to leave, bring them together in your garden, and hold them close.

---

*See chapter 8 for an exploration of Heaven's Garden.
†For more information on the Upward Draw, refer to *Healing Love through the Tao* (Rochester, Vt.: Destiny Books, 2005).

"See the love in their eyes, feel the love in your heart. Hear their words of fond farewell and speak your own, and that one day you will be reunited in a better place."

My throat swelled and tears welled. I gathered my children, as when they were young and before the times of alienation, my parents when they were old and after the times of alienation. We looked at each other, smiling, full of love, differences dissolved, the familiar smiles of those who know each other well and still keep love. It was, perhaps, the most beautiful moment of my experience. I could feel the healing and my mind went out to the shaman in gratitude for this last gift of love.

"And now," his voice grated newly rough as he paced between the deathbeds, "and now, look into the eyes of your loved ones, look deep, and then . . . " his voice rose before crashing down, "kill them! Give them the death you chose for yourself! Kill!" and then, softer, "keep looking in their eyes. See their faces change as they die, see their stares of disbelief, watch the horror happen as you destroy them, as you steal their lives, as they die before your eyes."

All around me the sounds of weeping as we mortals put to death those we held most dear, as we doled out death, as an empty dark anger infused my soul, as I stabbed my children in their little hearts, as I stabbed my parents, as I saw the disbelief and then the light fade from their eyes and even now I cannot not bring myself to describe the expressions on their faces had I words to do so.

I hate the shaman. I hate the shaman. I hate the shaman. The mantra reverberated around the walls of my brain. My fists clenched and shoulders tensed, I lay rigid in cold fury. My outer senses heard Tun Lo keening in the next deathbed, smugness shed. My family dead at my feet I thought to turn the knife on myself until the shaman's next words caught me up. "And now," he said, and his voice was gentle, "and now, bring them back to life!"

How could I unkill the dead? As if in answer—how many deaths had he facilitated to know our very thoughts—he said, "You took each life with the power of thought and with the power of thought you give it back. Look upon their faces as life flows back, see the light flooding into their eyes, their limbs moving again, the sound of their breath, the look of love and happiness on each face, their gratitude . . . "—gratitude?—" . . . for the appreciation of life you have restored."

Slogans of the New Age, nonattachment, detachment, empty mind, desire and aversion, floated like wraiths of the mind. This was the reality.

"Understand, now, how much more you love, honor, and value these relationships with your loved ones. They were lost and then found. How much more you appreciate what was lost when you find it. . . ." Words, words, words.

A life, or at least half my adult life, spent in self-development, self-improvement, learning the lessons, even teaching others, and now I had come face to face with myself as an angry, bitter individual, burning with resentment. Why, I had half a mind to just get up and walk out of that death house, pack my bags and leave.

I didn't even have the balls for that; just lay there seething with hatred as his empty words fell around me.

❂

The crashing bell woke me, along with screaming acolytes. "Wake up, wake up! Kneel, face the wall!" The bells rang and rang and the screams grew louder and louder. I struggled to sit up, groggy. "Face the wall! Kneel and face the wall!" Horrible loud voices screamed again and again. I fixed my blindfold and felt my way to the wall and knelt.

Silence fell. Everything before had gone like an unremembered nightmare, leaving its residue of terror. I had no reality, no anchor in consciousness. I was not me, I was nothing, I was scared. Time evaporated, senses dead.

A distant drum. Coming closer. Louder. A hammering on the door then howling banshees filled all space, shrieks, bells, gongs, drums shredding nerves.

The silence again, broken by hysterical sobs. And then the smell. Faint, far, a wisp of something so indescribably unpleasant that even now my stomach churns as I feel it closing in on me until it is right under my nose, pouring into my nostrils and I gag and try to move away but am held in place by demons. My gorge rises, vomit trickles down my chest. The smell fades leaving its traces on my skin.

Silence. Then a rattle, far away, closer and louder until deafening to my ears, and then, touched by feathered wings of the Angel of Death, I felt a piercing blow to my heart and fell back. Roughly they straightened me out, crossing my hands on my chest.

My body awaited the charnel cart. Those who had chosen burial were interred as the shaman recited the end of their mortal remains.

"Breath stops and pulses cease and blood is still. Bowels and bladder lose control. What was warm and living cools and stiffens. But nails and hair continue to grow in blissful ignorance for a while, until all systems stop. Skin slackens, muscles shrink, blood thickens, nerves end.

"As rot begins, your eyes fall in and hair falls out, brains go trickling down your snout. Guts dissolve into fragrant liquid. Little creatures enter by the soft parts, and start to feed and your dead body is alive with feasting parasites. Decay is slow, relentless, until only the bones remain.

"For those who chose to burn, the fire frazzles your hair and withers your skin and boils your blood. Brains expand to pop your skull. Your body roasts like barbecued pig then blackens, shrivels, and falls to ash.

> *All still, the fleeing soul departs*
> *Earth's debris for a better place,*
> *Wu Chi awaits!"*

A piped lament in the flowers of the forest sang me to my rest. Drumbeats, long and steady, on and on, for hours and hours, had I any sense of time, but I did not as I lay dead, without thought, undistracted, feeling nothing, wanting nothing, an empty city without buildings, the veil between the worlds ripped away to reveal no worlds, beyond the beyond, nothing.

I knew not how long they stretched the fabric of time that night or day or night and day but my body let me know it was not completely dead and sought to move but a squad of demons pinned me down. I embraced the pain and learned something. Some eons later another sensation reminded me of being, at some level, alive. When I could resist no more I sat up and moved to the end of my deathbed. I felt my hands taken and was assisted to my feet and led across a carpeted floor and then a cold, smooth-tiled floor, wet in places. The Red Angel's voice said, "Take off your blindfold when inside, switch on the light, off when you're finished. Then put your blindfold back on." She pushed me forward and the door closed behind me.

I used the toilet and did as she said, aware in a strange disassociated way of my physical body and its natural functions. I was led shuffling back to my deathbed where I lay in a state of nothing and must have slept.

❂

The sweetest music filtered through a slow consciousness. I was on my side, curled up, head on my arm, blindfold still in place. I became aware of movement around the room, whispering, sounds of people, doors opening. I did not risk another demon rush and lay quietly. How strange to notice the emptiness of my mind, freedom from thought, desire, action. Peace. Perhaps that which surpasseth all understanding?

A touch on my shoulder, encouraging me to sit up. Something was put in my hands, something small, delicate petals, nice to hold. The blindfold was peeled from my eyes and I found myself looking into the smiling brown eyes of Angel Rani. She wore flowers in her hair and a soft blue-colored sarong. "Welcome Home," she said and fastened the red thread around my wrist, then moved on to rouse another mortal.

Light filled the chamber, a chamber of life. Angels, demons, and acolytes gathered round the shrine on either side of the shaman, facing the Goddess, protector of the enlightened, terrifier of the ignorant. They embraced each other, human again, and tied the red threads around each other's wrists.

We were taken out into the grounds, into sunshine, and left until twilight, contemplating immortality, reunion with the Tao.

In the world of the shaman all time is now,
and when all time is now all space is one.

Spirit Guides

The nature of the shaman is to expand rather than to limit, and as the Tao describes the Way, however it may manifest, we give ourselves the freedom to explore and adapt all the ways of the known and the myriad mysteries of the unknown, from beyond the star nation above to the central sun below, to the hidden pathways within the fibers we call our brain and the moving mind in our blood. Finding or choosing a guide or being found or chosen by one gives us resources beyond our consciousness.

However we refer to them—as guardian angels, totems, guides, or spirits—they can come to us or wait around us. To access their guidance we can sit in meditation or take journeys through other worlds. We can draw cards or symbolic items from pouches. We can ask a wise one. We can journey in the physical world and see what or who comes up, resulting in our choosing or being adopted by a mentor from real life. We can ask a real person, past or present; popular choices are Lao-tzu, Confucius, Gandhi, and Mandela. A shaman of the Lakota Sioux declared the spirit of Elvis guided him.

When we take, choose, or are chosen by a guide we adopt a nature beyond our own. The guardians of the five elements, the immortals of the eight forces, and the twelve animals each have their nature. Teresa Lau writes of these in our tradition, while Jamie Sams describes those of Turtle Island in *Medicine Cards.* In the three sister traditions of Taoism, Native American, and Hindu/Tibetan, each creation has its spirit: even rocks are venerated as embodying the Divine.

USING THE MEDICINE WHEEL
TO ACCESS SPIRIT GUIDES

There are more ways to Spirit than buses to Trafalgar Square, limited to tradition or adaptable to your own practice, sitting cross-legged in cross-eyed meditation or googling the Divine (12,200,000 results). Guides in different forms appear in different sectors of the medicine wheel. For example, Fusion of the Five Elements introduces children who keep animals as their daemon spirits (like Lyra and Pantalaimon in Philip Pullman's trilogy, *His Dark Materials*). Both the children and the animals connect us to the elemental energies and the directions.

The early Taoists theorized that, like water, energy is formless. Without giving energy a form, it is difficult to capture its force. Just as water takes on the shape of the jar or pot that contains it, energy can take on the shape of the vessel into which it is placed. Regardless of the vessel's shape, the qualities of the water remain unchanged. Yet, by being contained in the vessel, it becomes easier to use. For example, because you can carry the water, you now can pour the water into a specific place. In doing so you are establishing a connection between the water and that place. The pictures and images of children and animals established by the early Taoists are similarly used to give form to pure energy in order to aid our connection to it.

Each of the children mentioned in the Fusion practices is associated with a color, an animal, and an organ of the body, all of which help us to envision the energy of the element.

The child of the east is in green, the color of the wood element. East is the place of the sunrise, the place where things begin. The animal of the east is Dragon.

The child of the north has two animals, Turtle and Deer, for north's dual role in conception and death, guarding the ancestral chi. The season is winter, when we tend to stay indoors, nights are longer, and the things to do relate to conception. With weather at its most harsh and food harder to come by, elder folk suffer and often choose this time to go to the lord of the north and their journey beyond. As turtle is one of the slowest creatures and spends much time in still-ness, it is an obvious candidate to represent death. Today we tend to look upon death as undesirable, don't talk much about it, and often do little to prepare for it, but it is perhaps the only event in life we can count on with certainty. Let's make friends with Turtle. Mindful that "your mood at the moment of death determines your next life," it is wise to stay cheery. Deer's quick movements show life. The horns remind us of readiness to create.

We muse over the different shamanic perceptions of the direc-tions. In the Native American tradition death is in the west. The sun goes down at the end of the "good red road" turning day into night. When it sets, the sun rises again, turning night back into day in a moment of celestial alchemy. For the Taoist the west represents the element of metal that, shaped into a weapon, can bring death. Tiger is the spirit of the child in white. Tiger's courage, speed, flexibility, and power give it dominance over all but Dragon. The two promote peaceful coexistence because if they fight, one dies and the other is crippled.

In the south flies the Firebird and the red child, spirit of love. The south is warm, friendly, and gracious. In ancient Sanskrit the south is dakhin, root of the word Dakhini, the rainbow-clad love sprite of the tantrikas.

The Golden Phoenix and the child in yellow mystify us with their power to rule the center, to appear between each season and to sit in the southwest. Their time is when the earth is golden and yields the harvest. And then the stalks are burned and the ash flies up on the wind before falling again, to nourish the earth. Phoenix is the mystery of the seventh direction, the shaman's lair: within!

Fusion of the Five Elements: Forming the Children and Their Animals

Pure Energy from the Kidneys Produces the Blue Virgin Child and the Deer

1. Bring your attention to the kidneys and the kidneys' collection point (shown in figure 8.1 as a small circle located at the perineum). Sense if the kidneys are cleansed of all negative emotion. This can be clearly indicated by a bright, illuminating blue color, or a strong feeling of calmness and gentleness. Spiral the kidneys' essence to their collection point until the collection point glows with bright blue light as the feeling of gentleness intensifies.

2. Once the intense, bright color and the sensation of gentleness peak, form the blue light into the image of a virgin boy or girl dressed in the blue color. This image represents the purest form of gentleness. Picture the boy or girl breathing out a blue breath. When enough of the blue breath accumulates, watch it transform into a beautiful Deer with antlers. The Deer represents a more refined, purer energy of the gentleness virtue. Make a

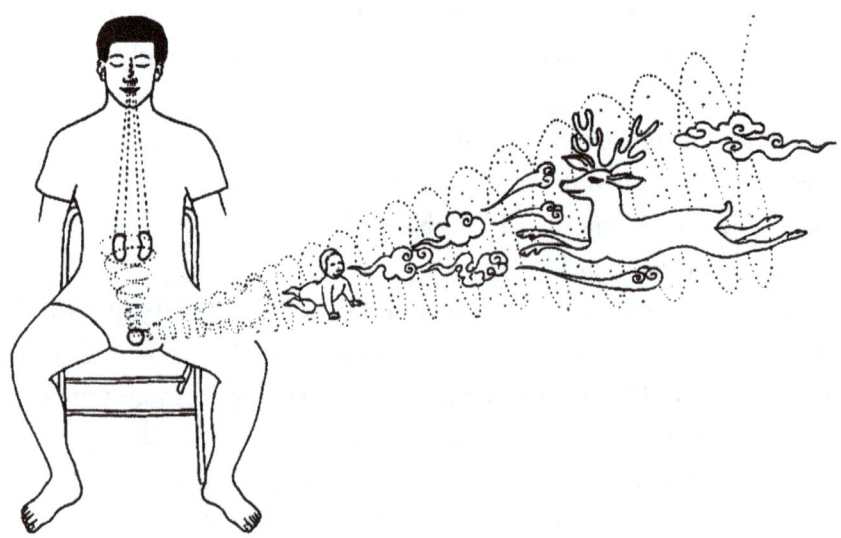

Fig. 8.1. Blue virgin child and Deer from the kidneys

strong connection with the blue virgin child and the Blue Deer, and instantly, at any time, you can restore a sense of calmness and gentleness within yourself (fig. 8.1). The brighter the colors, or the more intense the feeling of virtue, the purer the indication of virtue, and so, good health.

⚛ *Essence of the Heart Produces the Red Virgin Child and the Pheasant*

1. Be aware of the heart and its collection point (shown as a small circle). Picture the heart's collection point illuminating with bright, red light, and feel a strong sensation of love and joy, the virtues of the heart.
2. At the most intense moment of color and feeling, form the glowing red light into a virgin boy or girl, dressed in the red color. Watch the boy or girl breathe out a red breath, or sense the love, joy, and happiness. Form the breath or the feeling into a Red Pheasant.
3. Make a strong connection with the red virgin child and the Red Pheasant, and instantly, at any time, you can restore a sense of love, joy, and happiness within yourself (fig. 8.2).

Fig. 8.2. Red virgin child and Pheasant from the heart

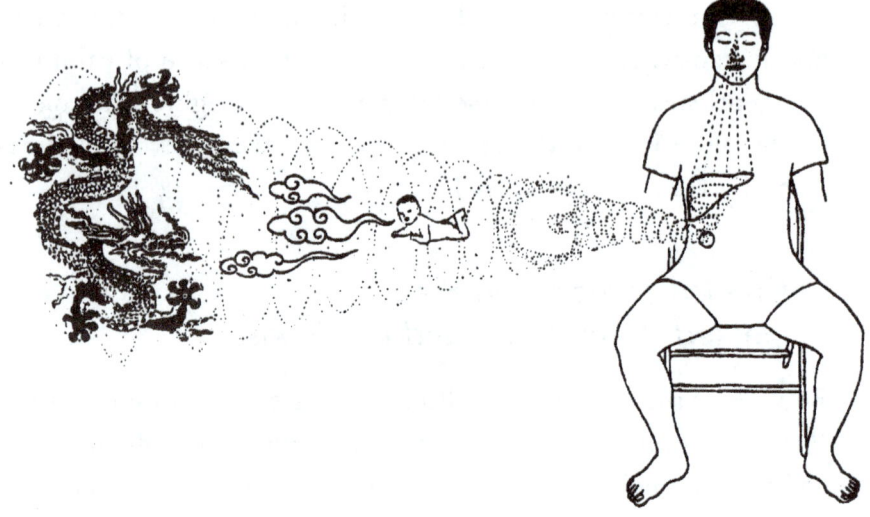

Fig 8.3. Green virgin child and Dragon from the liver

🌀 Pure Energy from the Liver Produces the Green Virgin Child and the Dragon

1. Concentrate on the liver and its collection point until you can picture the liver's collection point illuminating with a green light or feel an overwhelming sense of kindness.
2. When the green color is at its brightest, or when the feeling of kindness peaks, form the color or feeling into a virgin boy or girl wearing the color green. Watch the boy or girl breathe out a green breath, or feel the intense kindness, and form it into a Green Dragon.
3. Make a strong connection with the green virgin child and the Green Dragon, and instantly, at any time, you can restore a sense of kindness within yourself (fig. 8.3).

🌀 Lungs' Essence Produces the White Virgin Child and a Tiger

1. Be aware of the lungs and their collection point. Make the collection point luminous with a bright white or metallic color, or feel the powerful virtue of courage.

Fig. 8.4. White virgin child and Tiger from the lungs

2. When the vision of color or the sensation of courage is strongest, form it into a virgin boy or girl dressed in the color white. See the virgin boy or girl breathe out a white breath, or feel the sensation of intense courage. Change it into a White Tiger.

3. Make a strong connection with the white virgin child and the White Tiger, and instantly, at any time, you can restore a sense of courage within yourself (see fig. 8.4 on page 102).

❂ Pure Energy of the Spleen Produces the Yellow Virgin Child and the Phoenix

1. Concentrate on the spleen and its collection point at the front pakua. Observe as the spleen and the front pakua illuminate with a yellow light, or sense the strong feelings of openness and fairness.

2. When the color yellow or the feelings of openness and fairness are very intense, transform the color or feelings into a virgin boy or girl dressed in yellow. The virgin breathes out the yellow breath,

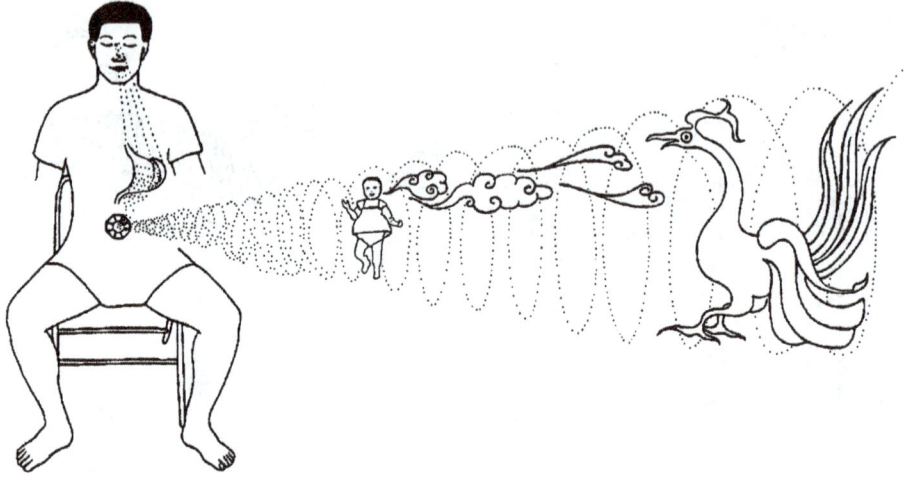

Fig. 8.5. Yellow virgin child and Phoenix from the spleen

or the feeling of openness or fairness increase, and the transformation of breath into a Yellow Phoenix occurs.

3. Make a strong connection with the yellow virgin child and the Yellow Phoenix, and instantly, at any time, you can restore a sense of openness and fairness within yourself (fig. 8.5). The brighter the colors, or the more intense the feelings of virtue, the purer the indication of virtue, and so, good health.

Use the Virgin Boy or Girl and the Animals to Form Protective Rings inside the Body

1. Beginning at the liver's collection point on the right side, with the virgin child and the Green Dragon, begin a circle up to the virgin child and Red Pheasant of the heart's collection point.
2. Then continue the circle around to the virgin child and the White Tiger at the lungs' collection point on the left side, and down to the virgin child and the Blue Deer at the kidneys' collection point.

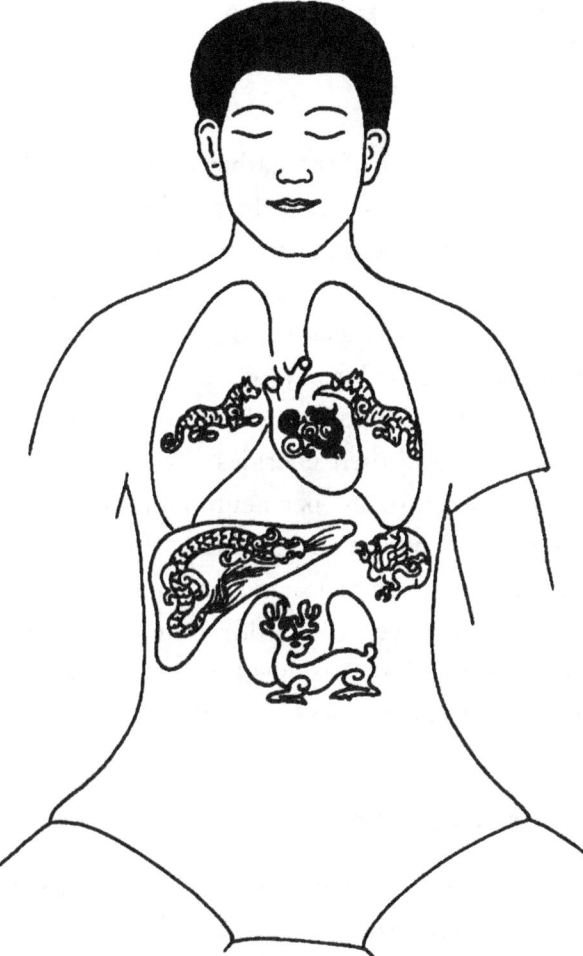

Fig. 8.6. Protective ring of the organs' power animals

The virgin child and the Yellow Phoenix are at the front pakua, which is in the middle of the four points of the circle.

These "power animals" form a protective outer ring around your organs (fig. 8.6). In the inner ring are your virtue energies, crystallized into the different colored virgin boys or girls.

❂ *The Pearl Connects with the Universal, Cosmic, and Earth Forces to Supply Energy to the Children and Animals*

The pearl will be the center of the gathering of the children and the animals and is enhanced by them. If the pearl dims or disappears, the children and the animals become hard to form.

1. Be aware of the pearl and feel it shine with the bright light of the silvery or bluish-white color of a pearl.
2. Be aware of the four pakuas, the organs' collection points, the organs, the senses, and their energies.
3. Move the pearl down to the perineum and into the Microcosmic Orbit. As the pearl moves through the Microcosmic Orbit, feel the universal, cosmic particle, and earth forces supplied to the pearl. As the pearl moves, the children and the animals can take energy from the pearl as they need it. This energy, in turn, will help to strengthen the organs physically and spiritually.

❂ *Finish the Meditation*

1. To finish, collect the energy, move the pearl into the cauldron, and spiral to condense the energy there.
2. Be aware of the animals and absorb them into the child to which each belongs: the Deer to the blue child, the Pheasant to the red child, the Dragon to the green child, the Tiger to the white child, and the Phoenix to the yellow child.
3. Be aware of the organs and the child belonging to each one: the blue child to the kidneys, the red child to the heart, the green child to the liver, the white child to the lungs, and the yellow child to the spleen. As you absorb the children into the organs, sense each organ illuminating with a brighter light. This bright light indicates a healthier organ containing a good energy.

Children of the medicine wheel dance around the center, open the box of balloons, and send the planets to guard the directions. The animals turn their faces to the sky and breathe the clouds of creation to seal the approaches. Animals and children are of the elemental energies, enabling all to share in the bounty of the Earth Mother.

FINDING GUIDES IN THE MUNDANE DIMENSION

Animal totems hold the power and the knowledge of being one with nature. They allow us to know life and commune with Spirit. As you walk the path of life certain animals may turn up to guide you for a time: a day, a week, sometimes a couple of months, or just a few hours. Some may be with you throughout your entire life, others until you no longer need them. Each animal has a special power and skill. The animal will make itself and its purpose known to you. Some may come to test you, manifesting fears you need to overcome. Learn the lesson: if you are in constant fear of something, accept the lesson. Animals come to us because they have a lesson to share; they remind us that we are part of the earth, with power and wisdom.

The following describes experiences that I (Kris Deva North) have had with spirit guides in the mundane world of everyday life.

The Story of Crow

I had my guides of the Five Elements that I placed around me, aware these were shared with many who walk in the Tao. On a journey in the real world I met a shamaness who read my Nine Totems using the Medicine Cards.* As well, I had an affinity with Snake, having shared my hut with one when I lived on the mountain. In that time, I also had other encounters

---

*These references pertain to specific aspects of the use of animal cards from the book and deck set by Jamie Sams and David Carson, *Medicine Cards* (New York: St. Martin's Press, 1999).

with Snake, such as when one slithered across the rocks to between my feet and licked my toes with its darting split tongue. Another wrapped the post of a hut I was visiting and followed me from one room to another. Another came, a whippy poisonous serpent of colors, during a storm fit to crack heaven while I was giving a healing treatment. So I adopted Snake, or Snake adopted me. I had Stoat, too, for a time, when my family life was like his.

Then, traveling in India, I was in the habit of drawing a card every day for guidance or inspiration. On twenty-seven days in succession I drew Crow. As I was practicing Tai Chi one morning on the roof of the Green Hotel in Dharamsala twenty-seven crows flew in, alighting on the parapet during my form. Crow became my totem that bade me walk my talk, a stern guardian reminding me how easy it was to fall back into the old patterns, to fall off the shamanic path. I met my beloved partner and showed her the Medicine Cards, spreading them out face down and mixing them around in a flat shuffle while telling the story of Crow, and saying, "It was as if I could pick any card on any day, and it would always be . . ." and I flipped a random card over and there it was again, "Crow!"

MAPPING THE WAY TO SPIRIT

Many are the ways to Spirit and the map is not the terrain. Each finds his or her own way. Take this resource as guidance if you need help starting. It describes the way down to Heaven's Garden, a passive scene from nature, the home of the children and animal totems encountered in Fusion of the Five Elements. The garden is itself a medicine wheel, with colors, shapes, sounds, scents, and directions. The way to the garden can be down the rainbow steps (see chapter 1) for those on the threshold of Taoist practice. For the adept, simply stepping through the inner eye takes her into this magical place.

The organic location of Heaven's Garden is that place where the five organs that comprise the medicine wheel in the human body are united, according to Kiiko Matsumoto and Stephen Birch. In their book *Hara Diagnosis: Reflections on the Sea*, they argue that the diaphragm, a web of connective tissue spanning the inner being from front to back and left to right, is the physical manifestation of the Triple Heater meridian. Touched by all the meridians on their internal and external routes, Triple Heater distributes the chi around the source points, taking conception energy from Heart Protector, a step-up transformer for the chi that initiated our being.

Exploring Heaven's Garden

First look around to become acquainted with the basic plan of the garden, the four directions and the center, the hub of the way to Spirit (see fig. 8.7 on page 108). This is where we can meet our first guides, the children and animals.

1. Enter the garden from the east, where things begin. Let it manifest: the green of plant life, healing forest, woodland, trees, shapes, textures of grass underfoot, bark of tree trunks, fresh fragrances, sound of cool breeze rustling leaves. See a grotto, from which the child in green emerges, leading a small Green Dragon. Spend time here, seeing the colors of nature, dappled light greening the boughs, feeling the textures, smelling the scents, listening to the sounds.

2. In the southern aspect, see the great red bushes of the rhododendron forest; feel the warm wind of the south; see the child in red emerging from the red grotto, Firebird on shoulder.

3. Ahead, in the center of the garden, see the beds of yellow flowers and the child in yellow emerging from the yellow grotto with the Golden Phoenix.

4. Beyond, in the west, amid the white rocks and white blossoms of the Zen garden, see the child in white with the White Tiger.

5. To the north, see a lake adorned with blue lilies, and the child in blue with Turtle and Deer.

6. In the center, amid the beds of yellow flowers, notice the pond fed by four streams, one from each direction.

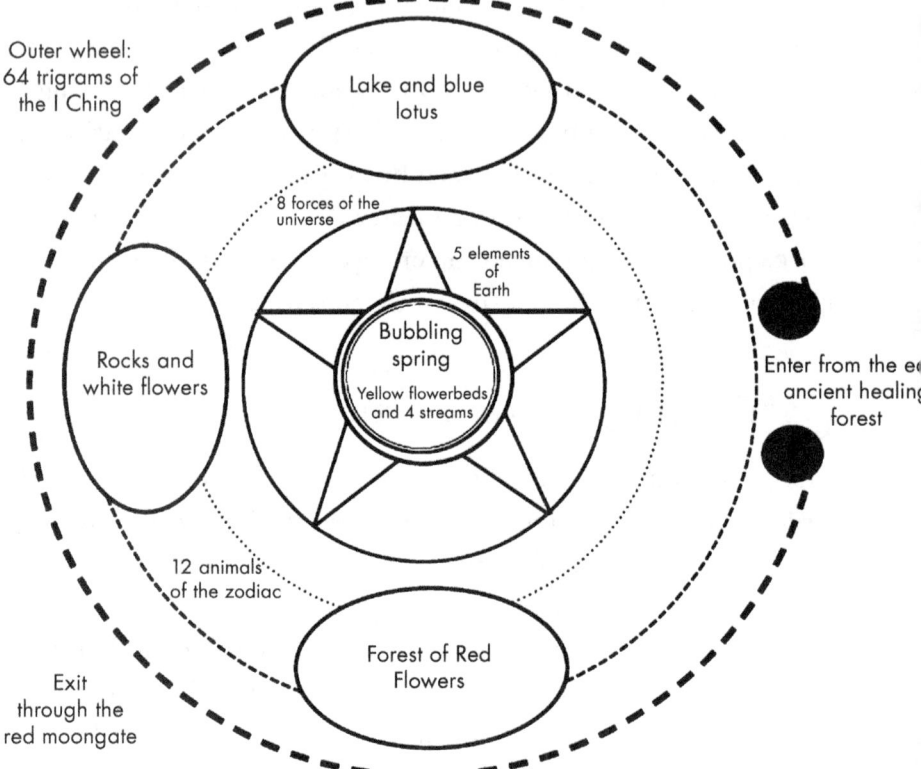

Outer wheel:
64 trigrams of
the I Ching

Lake and blue
lotus

8 forces of the
universe

5 elements
of
Earth

Bubbling
spring

Rocks and
white flowers

Yellow flowerbeds
and 4 streams

Enter from the e
ancient healin
forest

12 animals
of the zodiac

Forest of Red
Flowers

Exit
through the
red moongate

Fig. 8.7. Heaven's Garden

JOURNEYING TO MEET NEW SPIRIT GUIDES

Now we go a little further, to the worlds of above, below, and within. Again, it is the Triple Heater that forms the energy-network through its three levels of hot, warm, and cool. It is a special secret of Taoist shamanic practice that we seem to fly only in the celestial world. That is how other traditions perceive the Taoist shaman and we let them think so. But in fact the light of the pearl illuminates our journeys in the lower world and in the middle (or mundane) world of the human dimension, nature's plane, as well as in the upper world where the pearl helps us to absorb the light of Heaven. From the earliest we learned to store the pearl in our center. Now it is time to map the way to center on the path to Spirit.

Into the Yellow Chamber

We leave Heaven's Garden through the red moon-gate and enter into the Yellow Chamber of yin and yang through the orange door (fig. 8.8). There you will find manifestations of your own nature.

1. Pick tools and weapons from the right-hand wall, maps and guide-books from the left.
2. Directly in front of you you will see the back of a large comfort-able chair. Go around to seat yourself and notice the instruments set in the arms. One is marked "Time" and the other "Space."

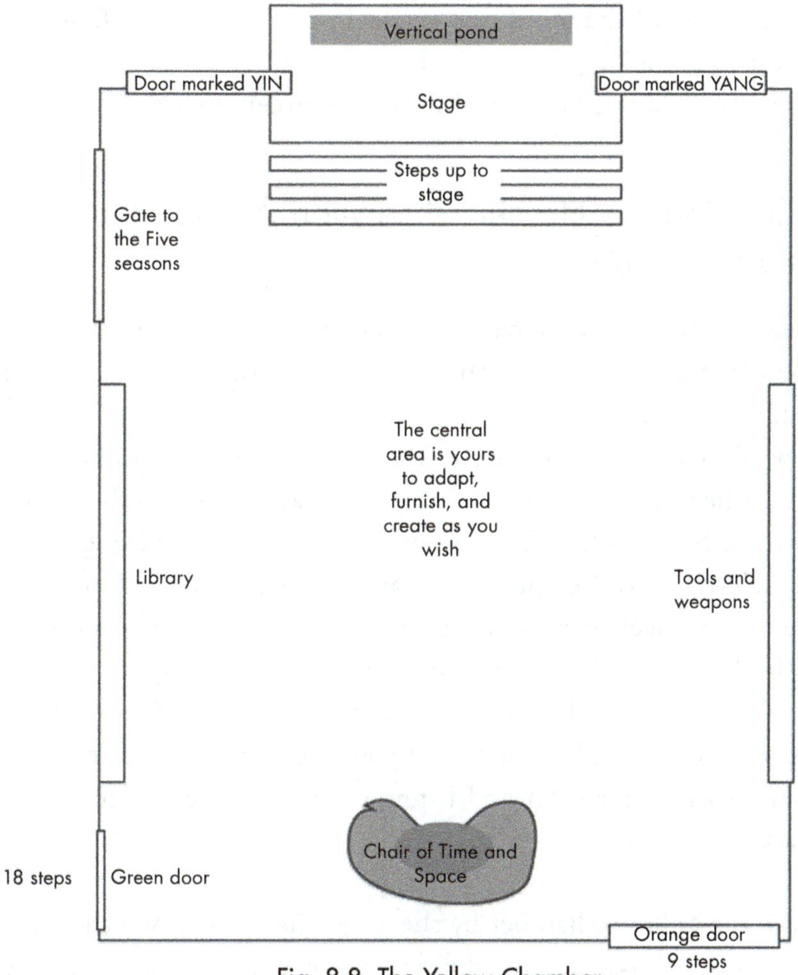

Vertical pond

Door marked YIN

Stage

Door marked YANG

Steps up to
stage

Gate to
the Five
seasons

The central
area is yours
to adapt,
furnish, and
create as you
wish

Library

Tools and
weapons

Chair of Time and
Space

18 steps   Green door

Orange door
9 steps

Fig. 8.8. The Yellow Chamber

3. At the far end of the left wall, open the Gate to the Five Seasons, a sliding door that reveals all the seasons: first a country scene, a land in springtime, buds bursting into bloom, and the fresh scent of spring in the air. The air warms under the sun as the seasons turn, a time to reap before the leaves grow heavy, colors turning gold and red until they fall to carpet the earth on a crisp cold day when the sun is bright but the breath makes clouds. Skeletal trees spike the dark white sky, opening its belly of snowflakes to blanket the world, settling until it is time to melt and fill streams and bring the land to life again.

4. From the Gate to the Five Seasons, turn to your right to look in to the screen of the mind, the vertical pond, mirror of life where mysteries unfold.

5. Leave the Yellow Chamber, through the green door on the left.

Entering the Higher Dimension through the Purple Court

After leaving the Yellow Chamber, you can go in search of other, more personal guides by exploring the Purple Court, the Temple of Spirit, and beyond.

How? Prepare while you are in the garden by thinking of a place and time where you want to be. You can travel in that ether from Auschwitz to Shangri-la, Washington to Xanadu. Or you can go randomly. Celestial travel employs the same principles as on Earth: go alone, or use a travel agent (a spirit guide). Backpack, or take a luxury tour as flights of angels sing you to your rest. Go at dawn to the bus station, dip churros in hot fortified coffee, follow the footprints of Hemingway. The Purple Court is all you want it to be, your place of communing with Spirit. Sit and listen, or sit in silence. Move or be still, walk or chew gum.

1. Leave the Yellow Chamber by the green door. Go down the steps to a passage, pass the blue door on the right, and then open the

second moon gate in the passage on the right to gain access to the Purple Court, the Temple of Spirit.

2. As you enter you may hear the sounds of Spirit, as you perceive Spirit to be. For you it may be chanted mantras, for others heavenly choirs; it can even be grunts of sensual gratification for those left behind by the Mayflower. In the Tantric tradition the Sanskrit seed sound of OM, pronounced "aah-ooh-mmm," is the sound of sexual climax, the moment equated by the Taoist to the sound of the creation of the universe, in the West innocently referred to as the big bang. You may hear the ringing of bells, beating of drums, growling of didgeridoos, electronic psych-trance, or voices of bliss or oasis. No matter—we each hold Spirit in our heart and reach it in our own way. Let the sounds reverberate and look to the writing on the wall.

3. Survey your temple, the Purple Court, and go to the wall. See the sacred glyph, the secret meaning of Spirit to you, and leap through a letter to the celestial realm. Have no fear, for here you soar between Heaven and Earth folded in the wings of the Divine.

We are fortunate to have the firsthand account of a female initiate, who was mentored on a journey to find her guides.

Pearl Is the Power, Pearl Is the Key

I thought him a handsome man with his short black triple-forked beard and wild hair bound in the red band of a trance-healer, a Master of the Formula. Their kind had no lineage and roamed alone, falling in fits and healing the sick. Rumors ran of gatherings under the black moon, circles of fire, and the calling of beasts. Mediator with Spirit, he held us in thrall with shadowed eyes of burning jet. A flick of his horsehair whisk could make people sleep and talk at the same time, walk on hot stones and feel no pain. Master of magic and fighting arts, always with a demon-killing sword strapped to his back, he tarried in the forest where villagers brought food and gifts to barter for healing and learning.

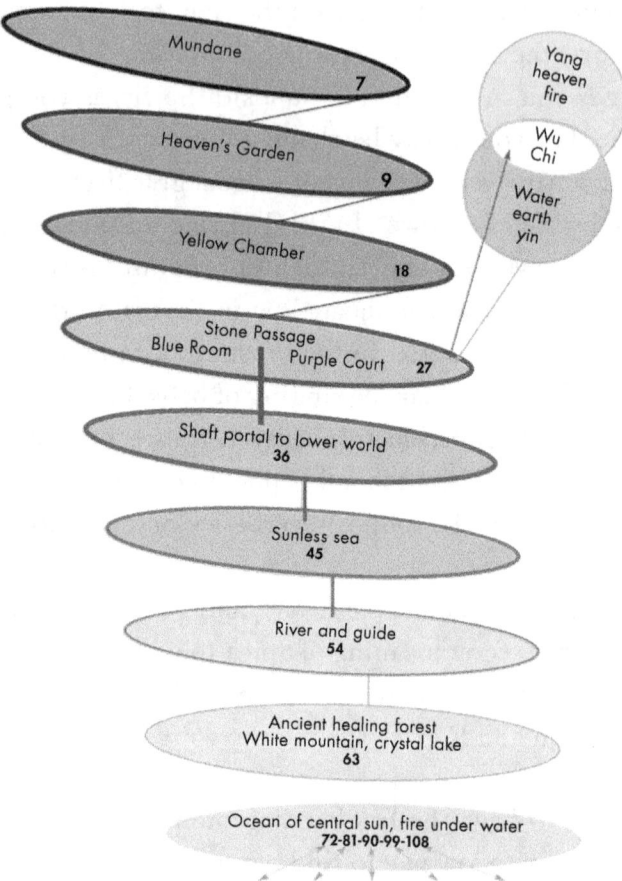

Fig. 8.9. The spiral journey through all the realms:
above, below, and within

He gave me a peach from his bag of fruit while he told of the days when the Fang Shih flourished, of the open teachings of the Lady, then of persecution by those who taught celibacy in defiance of the Goddess.

"Hidden masters, our influence waned. Now we hide and practice without drums, rattles, robes, or other articles of our craft, wearing the headband far from the cities. Now you cannot tell a sage by his clothes. But now we come again, to penetrate the inner courts."

He led me into trance. "With your mind's eye look in front of you and see the sun. Breathe in the sunlight; shine within. Shine within and now, look inward and upward to a point at the top of your head between skull and scalp. Between skull and scalp, pleasure's peak. From throbbing base it will surge to the crown! Hold it there, until the bolt of inner lightning strikes, down through your belly, down to spark the fire that opens the Jade Gate."

I had memorized the formula and rehearsed with discipline, awaiting the proper initiation but had no experience with which to understand it.

"Self-love is first love," said the Master, watching my slender fingers on the hooded bud glistening between my lips. "Self-intercourse, the union of yin and yang within one being, harmonizes the heavenly cycles, creating the immortal fetus, transcending the greater cycle of life and death."

❁

I fell into a dream, of him leading me over rough terrain, down into a strange valley. The path twisted through bushes beside a stream and took me into a cave. My bare toe struck a large stone disk, at least the length of my body across and a man's hand-span thick, with a hole in the center the size of my palm. It looked like a huge coin, with a slightly concave surface carved in a curious pattern, the outline of a Dragon in low relief surrounded by etched characters. I read, "East, where things begin."

I knew these words, the opening incantation. "The season is springtime, the element Wood, the guardian Dragon."

Similar stones were scattered in a circle, as if fallen from the pouch of a giant. In the center lay a triangle of three.

The next stone, to my left, spoke. "The season is summer, the direction south, the element Fire," and in it the guardian Firebird was carved.

My hair stood on end as I looked around, peopling the stones with sages in silken robes and shifted shapes, the eight immortals and gods of the left and right, human monsters and beast-headed angels, Turtle and Deer from the kingdom of north, the place of death and conception, White Tiger prowling the west, and Golden Phoenix soaring above.

There were nine stones, the number of completion: one in the center, with three around it: ching, chi, and shen—the Three Treasures! I caught my breath. The outer stones made a five-pointed star for the elements. The five and the three made the eight forces, with the one in the center completing the nine.

The center stone was blank, a smooth disk except for the hole: Wu Wei, the void. I lay down on it, imagining myself a sacrifice. It began to spin, faster and faster. A crescendo of pleasure rose to bliss, the gate to ecstasy opened, wide and welcoming. Then a mighty wind tore through and a crack of thunder split the valley. Flying in space, I spread among the stars, the Milky Way streaming from my loins. I came to the white mountain reflected in a crystal lake, ancient healing forest around the shore. The sun went down, fire under water, boiling the ocean to steam, dissolving my body to light.

○

I awoke at the top of seven broad white steps down to a garden. Statues stood here and there. Two conical bushes with dark green shiny leaves marked the entrance. I went through. To my right stretched a lake, blue lilies floating, as far as the eye could see. Ahead of me a lawn path was flanked by beds of yellow chrysanthemums. Beyond, there were spirals of pebbles round a rocky mound, with trees of white blossom. To the left of the entrance bloomed a forest of rhododendrons, transforming into a mountain smoking at the summit. Liquid red rock overflowed the slopes, formed pearly skin, and poured into the lake in thick clouds of steam. The smell of sulfur pervaded, until a sudden strong wind cleared the air and all was as before.

Amid the yellow flowers, flush with the ground, a shallow bowl of liquid simmered, fed by streams from the four directions. "Where are the statues?" With this thought, they appeared beneath the boughs of a tree.

A beautiful young god, whose green mantle became a tail as he shifted into the shape of a Dragon, took me through flowered pathways, past the simmering spring to the raked pebbles around the rockery of white bushes. The Dragon breathed fire into a grotto. A young girl materialized, dressed in white, white flowers in her dark hair. Her voice was sweet and musical.

"Close your eyes and focus on the breath coming and going through your nose." The familiar words comforted me. "With your mind's eye look in front of you and see the sun. Breathe in the sunlight; shine within, inward and upward to a point at the top of your head, between your skull and your scalp. Feel it grow warm, and let that warm relaxing feeling flow down, down through your body, to the base of your being.

"Breathe in through Hui Yin, the Gate of Life and Death [at the perineum]. Draw the essence into the lake of yin, and up your spine to the lake of yang in the crown. Blend it with sunlight and circulate in the Microcosmic Orbit, transcending life and death."

I felt myself becoming light-headed. It passed and a sense of courage filled me with each breath.

"Create the empty force," the girl's voice continued, "pull in your belly without taking in breath. Imagine sucking in through your sexual organs."

Power surged up inside me, stronger than pleasure. Unasked, unbidden, my eyes flashed open. A White Tiger sat where the girl had been, staring at me with eyes of light. I closed my lids at once, feeling I had seen something forbidden, and my flesh rose in tiny bumps.

A brahmin priest and a wild man in rags appeared.

"I am Fire," the wild man laughed, "Liago, fire of warmth, fire of destruction."

"Earth am I," sang the brahmin, "Serenity."

"Metal, me." The Tiger-girl appeared before me. "I reflect and inspire, I cut and contain."

"And I am Wood, guardian of the east, where things begin." It was the beautiful young god in the green cloak.

We walked in silence to the lake. Blue lotus patched the surface. I could see pebbles under the clear water. The girl faced north and called, "Lord of the north, come forth!"

A ripple in the lake became a wave, the water heaved and opened and a great Turtle splashed to the shore trailing clumps of lotus, ridden by a woman whose clinging wet blue dress outlined her every contour.

"Kanpani am I. Water," she said in a deep voice, sliding off its back.

They all joined hands in a circle around me and guided me to the thermal pool fed by four hot streams. I felt myself dissolve in boiling liquid, reducing, thickening, condensing into crystal, spinning into translucent pearl containing the rainbow, hurtling to the center of all existence, time abolished . . .

Tiger-girl stood at the foot of the seven stone steps, framed white between the dark green shrubs. She carried weapons of pearl, sword at waist, round shield slung over her arm, and, in her right hand a strange object the shape of a short blunt arrow. I started toward her with a smile but she backed away, beckoning me to follow, until we stood some twenty or so paces apart, under the trees.

I had expected a welcome. The garden was my refuge and my strength. Was it failing me?

"Where are the others?" I said.

In reply, she hurled the thunderbolt. I tried to leap aside. "Stand still," she yelled and my legs froze. The missile spiraled right through my chest. No pain. I stood in shock, grief cascading from my lungs. It buzzed back to her hand: she aimed and threw again. It struck between my eyebrows and opened my brain. A third burst my belly. I fell flat and another ripped between my legs and split me to my crown. The night sky flooded my being and now the very stars rained down, piercing my ribs in a hail of light.

Tiger-girl shook the weapon high, changing it to a weighted string she whirled above her head as she danced in space toward me, shouting:

"I hurl the pearl, I whirl the pearl
Drill your body, cut your bones."

The first cut severed my neck, the next my shoulder blades, then hips, knees and elbows, wrists and ankles. Still howling and whirling she danced around, weighted string whirring, slicing every joint of my spine from Jade Pillow to tail.

Disembodied, I floated, a skeleton apart. The Tiger snarled and birthed a Turtle that shape-shifted into Kanpani, hammering my bones with breath of ice. They clattered to earth, to a glade in the ancient healing forest, where Wood in his green mantle soothed me back to wholeness.

Steam dissolved grief from my lungs and impatience from my heart, fear from my kidneys, and worry from my spleen. I steamed my spine, renewed my bones, and breathed blood into bone marrow. I steamed my glands, restored my link with Heaven above, Earth below, and the world around.

But when those easy jets of steam reached my liver they hit raging anger that would not dissolve, melt, or yield but instead transformed into power, the power of green shoots bursting rock, the power of springtime: birth, growth, and renewal.

The steam condensed, rivulets running down inside my flesh, dripping into darkness, drop by cool drop, into a familiar void . . . on stone, far below.

Something lay beneath the garden.

"It is another world," said the brahmin, "neither lower nor higher, nor Earth nor Heaven. Your body lives anchored in the mundane. To travel at will means learning to find—or create—the portals and pathways. Within each world is another. That third world you sensed below is neither third nor below, but your human mind needs a sense of time and space to understand it. The truth is, all time is now and all worlds are one. A season here is a heartbeat there. With each world you master, your power increases and mind expands until you become the rare one who can step lightly in all.

"But be aware! You cannot meet yourself in one world. You can be in two worlds in the same moment but not two moments in the same world."

"What would happen?"

"Only the gods know. The teaching says your existence would be erased on Earth, your history deleted from the annals of Heaven, but 'there are more worlds in Heaven and Earth than dreamed of in our philosophy.' Now you go where you've never been. You must know the return, to come back of your own volition should you meet danger. Go left behind, return right."

He waved his arm down my front as if brushing something off and a sudden calm settled in me.

"Look around you," said Wood, "the colors, the shapes." I saw trees rearing to a sky of sunless blue, green leaves and dappled light, hanging vines, trunks of silver, roots like huge fins, groves of palms and bamboo clumps, flowers of red, yellow, and white.

"Hear the sounds of nature," murmured Kanpani as wind bent bamboo and rustled leaves. A branch cracked. A coconut fell with a thud and did not bounce. I shuddered. Water rushed over stones (see fig. 8.10 on page 119).

"Smell the fragrance," whispered Tiger-girl and scent of jasmine filled my nostrils.

The brahmin said, "Touch the textures." I stooped and rubbed my hands on the earth, pulled a clump of grass and rolled it in my palm. I picked a flower to stroke its petals and snapped off a stem of bamboo.

And from Liago, "Close your eyes, curl back your tongue, and taste the dew." The night sky opened: my mouth filled with sweetness.

"Take this, the pearl of compassion." Something round and smooth filled the palm of my right hand. I folded my fingers over it. "This is your key, your sword, shield, and armor, the light of Heaven to shine in all worlds. When you see the gate, go through with it."

They counted down the rainbow, chanting the colors and the numbers from seven to one. "Now you are at the deepest and most inward level of your being, deeper and more inward than ever before."

A great whirling vortex sucked me to Heaven and flung me to Earth, lightning split a starless sky, the mountain erupted and the lake boiled over, the sea evaporated and the sun went out. I tumbled into the void.

❂

"Look over your left shoulder."

Left behind! I saw a red moon gate in the trunk of an ancient tree. My stomach somersaulted. The pearl pulsed in my hand: Go now! I launched myself through the gate, landed on my feet at the top of a flight of steps spiraling down into darkness. Shining the pearl ahead of me I took them at a rush, counting down as fast as I went. At nine I slammed into something solid. I aimed the pearl to see what. The light bounced off a blank orange door. I stood, nonplussed.

"Trust your destiny. Use your will." Gripping the pearl between forefinger and thumb, I thrust it forward like a key.

The door swung inward and yellow light flooded a spacious chamber, walls to left and right lined with shelves of scrolls, a door each side and the spaces between hung with tools, implements, armor, and weapons. All this I took in with a glance but my eyes stopped at the seeming impossible: the end wall was not a wall but a vertical pond, bordered with rocks, orange, and gold fish lazily swimming up, down, and sideways beneath a still

Fig. 8.10. Ancient healing forest

surface that reflected me and the room. With no trace of a ripple two men stepped out from the pond and stood, perfectly dry, on the stone floor.

I looked again, over my left shoulder and saw a green moon gate where, I was certain, none had been before.

"Go down the steps, along the passage backward."

"Backward?"

"Run forward, count backward. Ignore the two doors on your right. At the count of one is a round stone with a ring in it, set in the floor. Lift the stone and jump."

Green fumes billowed from an open shaft. I landed in a vaulted cavern measureless to man, with a lake, still and smooth, a boat on the strand. I could not see the cave roof. The walls rose like arching cliffs. I could make out vague giant shapes of immortals, human and animal, towering in the walls. They seemed alive, indeed the only sign of life. The lake lay vast and opaque as if waiting to be walked on.

The boat, a hollowed log with pointed ends, had an eye burned each side of the bow. I got in; the pearl became a paddle. I tried different ways to make it work, got the hang of it, and headed toward a speck of light.

Digging deep to go skimming along I learned to give each stroke time to take effect and soon floated out on the river. The sky, dull purple, seemed lower than had the roof of the cavern. I liked the feeling of power from sending the boat shooting along. I realized I hadn't worked out a way of stopping. A moment of anxiety . . . I needn't have worried: this was a different world.

The little boat slowed. I scanned ahead. A broad ditch sloped down to join the river from the right. The boat bumped its nose on the bank. From what looked like distant snow I saw two figures running toward me, a man in a fur hood, a wolf loping at his side.

The face in the hood was broad and flat with slits for eyes: I could barely see them until he came close and then I gasped at the startling violet of their color. The wolf stretched like a dog, and sat.

They guided me beyond the ocean of the central sun, through caves of lost souls, past fragments of hovering spirit, through portals past, to meet my Nine—of left and right, the four directions and the fifth above, the sixth below, and the secret seventh, within—who are with me now and always.

And then he brought me back, over my right shoulder to the narrow river beneath the purple sky, the cavern measureless to man, over the lake opaque to the silent shore, beneath the shaft.

There I shut my eyes, bent my knees, took a deep breath, held my nose with one hand, the pearl tight in the other and jumped as high as I could to get through those acrid green fumes. My eyes stung: I had to open them when I hit the passage floor and scrabbled for the ring in the stone. There! I looped the pearl through, lifted and swung it back into place.

Along the passage, passing the doors to ignore, to the flight of steps, shining my pearl as I bounded up and burst through the green moon gate into the chamber. With my pearl key, I hurtled through the orange door, dived through the red moon gate into the garden and rolled across the grass.

This initiate's story is reminiscent of the immortals Ho Hsien-Ku and Lu Tung-Pin. She would not reveal her nine guides, saying it was for each to find their own. (According to Mircea Eliade, who wrote

Shamanism: Archaic Techniques of Ecstasy, if you see a guide four times, bring it home.) Her story also reminds us of the centrality of the pearl for the Taoist shaman:

- In the moment of ecstasy, instead of sending the blast of light inward, the shaman draws the pearl from the cauldron and projects it from the crown.
- In the moment of ecstasy the shaman shoots the pearl through the inner eye to Heaven's Garden.
- In the moment of ecstasy the shaman shoots the pearl through a letter of the word on the wall in the Purple Court.

The pearl is the consciousness of the shaman. Pearl and shaman are one.

WORLD OF SPIRIT

Where is the world of Spirit? When workmen came to renovate the chapel they wore cement-crusted boots and smoked cigarettes. The chaplain said they were close to God in their own way and we ought not expect others to worship as we do. That lesson sank in early. A Western traveler riding the desert around Pushkar went, after a short rest in the shade of a tamarind, to use a big stone as a mounting block.

"Wait," cried his groom, "do not step on God."

Omar Khayyam reckoned the tavern as good as the temple and justified many a life of aberrant worship.

The monk in Thailand was heard to lament, "In this town the taverns are full and the temples empty."

> *Be aware! You cannot meet yourself in one world. You can be in two worlds in the same moment but not two moments in the same world.*

Comparison with Other Traditions

Prehistoric peoples migrating from the central Asian plateau carried their traditions and practices to the four directions: north to Siberia, west toward Europe, east to China, and south to India. Some ventured to the cold northeast and what is now Alaska, then south through what we call the Americas, taking some 20,000 years to reach the southern tip, Tierra del Fuego.

Later migrations, reverse migrations, wars and alliances, trade and exchange, all contributed to cross-cultural fertilization of the old ways as they became new ways in their relevance to modern life. Common threads run through all the ancient practices, with minor variations in concept or color. For example, the Native American tradition is remarkably close to the Taoist in a number of ways, such as the worship by smoke and purification by sweat, though the Native Americans use a peace pipe rather than incense stick, and their sweat lodge is more portable and so more suitable for nomadic peoples than the Taoist hot tub, which requires permanent construction and is much more fuel-hungry.

The dragon appears globally, though with different attributes. In the northern European tradition the dragon lives in caves, guarding quantities of gold and demanding a diet of virgins to dissuade it from terrorizing the locals until some young wannabe comes along and slays it, thereby adding himself to the celebrity A-list. The patron saint of England, St. George, was one such dragon slayer. The Western dragon's bad press, in the words of Vinod Solluna, "is largely the result of quite a few thousand years of a systematic and quite deliberate Judaeo-Christian propaganda war against The Old Ways." The Book of Revelations personifies Babylon as a whore seated on a dragon, condemning the city as "the Mother of Harlots and of the Abominations of the Earth." One of the first conquerors of the Old Ways was St. Patrick, famous for "driving all the snakes out of Ireland."

One story that unites the traditions all the way from North to South America is that of Quetzalcoatl, the feathered serpent (a more poetic rendering of "dragon"). Two countries in the modern world display a dragon on their national flag: Bhutan is the representative from the East, with Wales in the West. In India the god Shiva is the dragon god. Across the world in China the dragon evolved as a deity through accumulation of the parts of various totems and was gifted with magical powers, becoming the symbol of the Son of Heaven, the emperor on the dragon throne.

THE MEDICINE WHEEL AROUND THE WORLD

Most appropriate for comparison in our context is the medicine wheel with its directions, colors, symbols, and animals. Two traditions on opposite sides of the world are comparable to that of China: the stone circles of Northern Europe, of which the most famous is Stonehenge in England, standing in all its permanence, and the medicine wheels of North America.

Stonehenge is aligned with the two solstices. Midwinter is hard even with the comforts of modern technology and the winter solstice festival is still maintained, reminding us of atavistic yearnings. In olden times rural folk, whose stockpiled food was running low, turned to the dying sun that had so blessed them in summer. In a constructive effort that rivals the pyramids, they built a medicine wheel, a

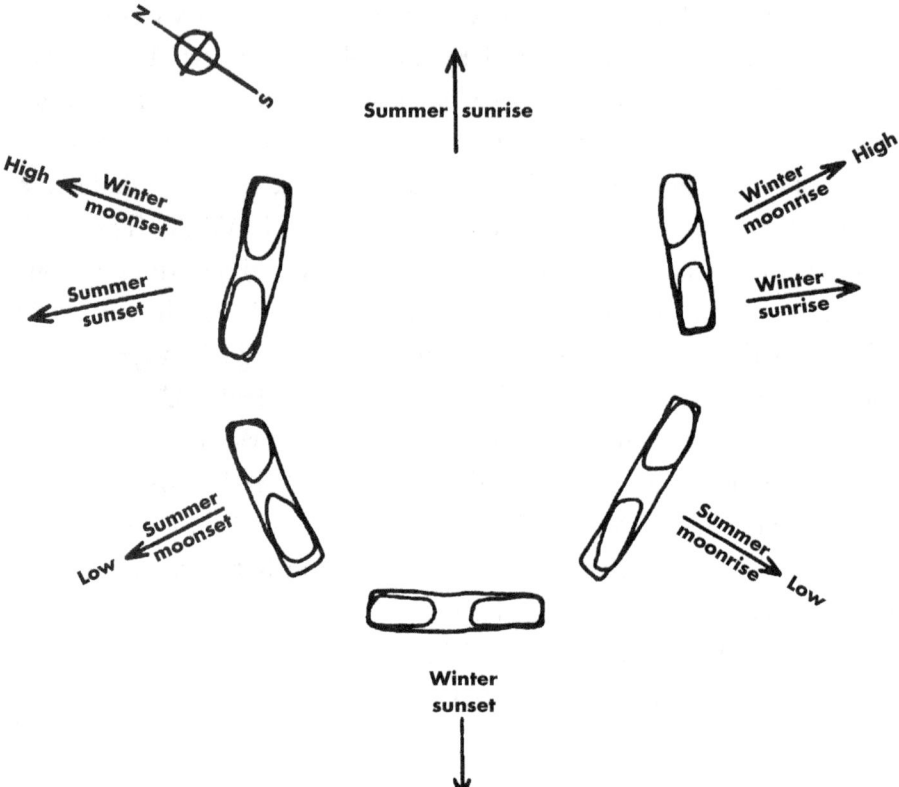

Fig. 9.1. Alignment of Stonehenge with rays of the sun and the moon

circle of life, to catch the sun at its zenith, the summer solstice, and revive it at its nadir (fig. 9.1). From the winter solstice on, things could only get better.

In the Native American tradition directions and sections vary among tribes. All follow the principle that life is a circle with north, south, east, and west, Mother Earth below, Father Sky above, and Spirit within, for the medicine wheel is a physical manifestation of spiritual energy. The wheel made it clear that we are all connected to "all our relations": we two-leggeds; plant life; the "standing people" (stones); the "sitting people" (keepers of the records of our planet); and the four-, six-, and eight-leggeds, each with a part to play in mutual existence.

The wheel cycles through changing seasons; as we evolve, we change like the seasons, learning from each other and all our relations. As humans we are part of Earth, children of the Mother, part of Spirit. Native Americans recognize the power of the animal spirits by wearing skins, painting them on walls, asking Spirit to guide the hunt, and blessing the spirit of the animal. They link to the animal guides and their power, remembering that we too are animals with spirit. Spirit has put all of us together, and given us medicine for the body and the spirit.

CALLING THE DIRECTIONS

*With grateful thanks to John Mark Eggerton
of San Francisco, California*

A selection of medicine wheel directions and their various attributes as seen by different traditions reveals similar themes, even though the attributes and sequence may vary. Wiccan and Native American traditions favor following the directions sunwise: east, south, west, north, and back to east. In the Celtic Druid tradition, elements may be called sunwise (clockwise) during the male part of the year (Beltane through Samhain), and moonwise (counterclockwise) during the female part of the year (Samhain through Beltane). Beltane and Samhain are the most important holidays in the Druid tradition. Beltane is a celebration of life, sex, energy, and the joy of living. Samhain is a celebration of the lives of those who have gone before us, a time to honor the memories in our hearts of the great ancestors of blood and tribe who watch over us and speak in our dreams, and our recent beloved who have passed.

There are times when an antisunwise order may be used, especially in some shamanic and Norse practices. Going antisunwise doesn't necessarily mean negative magic; it could for instance, symbolize reversing negativity, and is often used in defensive and banishing rituals. The Norse traditionally begin their year at Yule, the winter solstice and longest night of the year, a symbol of darkness turning to light. Many shamans go into darkness specifically to find the light.

CHEROKEE TRADITION		
DIRECTION	**COLOR**	**QUALITY**
East	Red	Victory, success
South	White	Peace, happiness
West	Black	Death
North	Blue	Turmoil, trouble, defeat
Above	Yellow	Sun, spirit
Below	Brown	Earth, fertility
Center	Green	Nature, life

General Pagan Tradition

In the general Pagan tradition, each direction has several attributes, including human values, time of day, human aspect, element, animals, colors, and others.

East: Place of illumination and enlightenment. Dawn. Spirit. Air, the winds. Birds and all flying creatures. Yellow. Red. Purple (Celtic). Breath. Sword.

South: Place of learning, faith, and trust. Noon. The mind, intellect, and mental processes. Fire, lightning, volcanoes. Serpents and reptiles. Red. Yellow. Green. White (Celtic). Dragon. Raven. Salamander. Anger.

West: Place of strength and introspection. Dusk. Emotion. Water, rivers, lakes, oceans, rains. Fish, frogs, turtles, and all creatures that live in or close to water. Black. Blue. Pale (Celtic). Moon. Wells.

North: Place of wisdom and experience. Midnight. Physically grounded energy. Earth, the element binding all elements together, minerals, the roots of plants and herbs. Creatures that live underground. White. Black (Celtic). Treasure. Pentacles.

Center: Place of essence and truth. Home of the Great Spirit who resides in every human heart.

KONDRATIEV CELTIC SYMBOLISM

DIRECTION	TREASURE/ TRIBAL FUNCTION	ANIMALS	OTHERWORLD CITY
East	Cauldron, plenty	Salmon	Muirias (fort of the sea)
South	Stone, song	Land stag (summer), boar (winter)	Failias (stone of Fal)
West	Spear, knowledge	Boar (summer), stag (winter)	Goirias (burning fort)
North	Sword, battle	Eagle	Findias (bright white fort)
Center	High king	Sovereignty	Failias (stone of Fal)
Southwest	Direction of the Goddess	Sow	Failias (stone of Fal)

In this Celtic tradition, fire and summer are represented by incense on altars and water and winter are represented by salt on altars.

Unitarian Universalist Pagans' Celebration

1. We greet the east, direction of the element of air, traditional quarter of the intellect, the mind, the power to know. May we all make learning a lifelong endeavor, both for its innate joy and as a means to help the world of which we are all a part.

   We greet the east, direction of air: gentle breezes and strong winds, realm of the beauty of clouds and birds, bearer of the weather that touches us all, the breath of life we inhale and exhale. We are a part of all around us.

2. We greet the south, direction of the element of fire, traditional quarter of energy. May we all aspire to be channels of energy with the power to create, to act, to be agents of beneficial change.

   We greet the south, direction of fire: candle flame, bonfire, starlight, and sunlight, the energy that warms us and gives life to the world we inhabit, the energy that pulses along our nerves. We are a part of all around us.

3. We greet the west, direction of the element of sea and water, traditional quarter of emotions. May we all have courage to face our feelings, to share our joy with others, to learn empathy and compassion from our sorrow, to direct our anger into constructive efforts.

   We greet the west, direction of water: rain, snow, rivers, and lakes, the great encircling ocean from which all life first came, the blood that flows through our veins still bearing the saltiness of that original home. We are a part of all around us.

4. We greet the north, direction of the element of earth and stone, traditional quarter of the body. May we draw strength and adapt-ability from this quarter and a deep, abiding respect for the vast web of the earth.

   We greet the north, direction of earth: metal and stone, hill and valley, Mother who bears and nourishes all life—root and leaf, fur and feather and scale and skin, muscle and bone and brain cell. We are a part of all around us.

All traditions teach the same truths in their own ways.

Creating Power Fields

THE NATURE OF POWER FIELDS

In this ever-changing world we live in, where energy and matter, wave and particle, create our reality, power occurs in nature or is human-made. The energy field of our planet holds the moon in place, while the energy field of the moon moves tides on Earth. In our struggle to master unmasterable forces, we turn to nature. Archimedean screws raised water to nourish crops. Huge modern devices rolled by waves or turned by wind replace fossil fuels. Power, so familiar in daily life, seems strange and mysterious in the context of shamanic practice.

Fill your gas tank, switch on your electric light, power moves your car or illuminates your home. Your computer has power to access the Worldwide Web. When a utility company bills you for power this is perfectly normal and you may use its power to go online and pay.

Are power and energy the same? Or is power an application of energy?

Our ancestors accessed the energy fields of what they perceived as the Divine, building pyramids and steeples. On the pyramid they may have torn the hearts from living beings to harness the power of the Divine, or prayed and chanted in temples. They built medicine wheels such as Stonehenge to connect with the power of sun and moon. And each of us has the ability to create his or her own power.

A power field is a bubble of reality separate from but part of the dimension of the present. Moving hands together and apart generates an antimagnetic field that you can physically feel between the palms. We can develop, expand, and direct the field so the bubble changes from more or less spherical to linear. A healer might use this to enhance the energy field or aura of a patient. A martial artist might use it to disrupt the energy field of an opponent, or to concentrate, direct, and focus his own.

Shamanic power comes from the ability to create energy fields that transcend time, space, and physical boundaries accepted as normal in the mundane dimension. Walking on fire, the practitioner creates an energy field that protects the physical body from burning or even feeling the heat.

A power field can be external or internal. Cosmic Healing techniques* describe protocols for setting up power fields around self and patient, and guiding a patient to set up her own. The Pearl of Fusion is a typical internal power field.

Ann's experience illustrates the importance for the Taoist shaman to protect herself by setting up an energy field to guard against contamination or depletion. Ann worked in a hospice for the dying. Her clients often did not make it to the next appointment. These souls—about to embark on their journey from the mundane, with energy fields atrophied by years of pain and suffering, each sharing the thought of the Fifth Patriarch on his deathbed, "I don't want to go"—would sense Ann's shining clear aura, and want some of it, all of it, any of it. They would suck like dementors to cling on a little longer. In the course of her healing journeys Ann learned a brief form of protection. It is a temporary measure (no substitute for a daily practice of meditation or surrender to the Divine), a temporary power field.

In the moment before encountering a patient, she sits or kneels and raises both arms, palms to Heaven, letting Heavenly chi flow

---

*Cosmic Healing techniques are detailed in *Taoist Astral Healing* (Rochester, Vt.: Destiny Books, 2004) and *Taoist Cosmic Healing* (Rochester, Vt.: Destiny Books, 2003).

down. Lowering her arms, she extends them either side in a downward sweeping half-circle, palms facing Earth. Then she draws Earth chi up by bringing her palms together, completing the circle at the navel energy center.

It is that simple. No thought, nor prayer, nor incantation, only intention. But it sets up her energy-field with a vibration that is different from that of the patient, as if she could "sit inside the patient's mouth and be untouched."

USING MEDICINE WHEEL AND SPIRIT GUIDES TO CREATE POWER FIELDS

Rather than being a scholastic essay from history or a repetition of alleged formulas, the guidelines below are intended for your own practice. Arcane terminology filtered out, we present a simple how-to guide, amplified by descriptions of practice and illustrated by stories of real experience.

 ## Creating Your Personal Power Fields

 ### Creating the Wheel of Earth

Choose your spot to create the Wheel of Earth. It can be indoors or outside. The only restrictions are those you put on yourself or put upon you by the "spirits of place" (the yin of the Mother Earth and the yang of Heaven, and any local spirits who may have an interest in what goes on in their territory). Spirit will always guide you: accept! And be aware. When it is your time to find your space, be open to feelings, sounds, sights, and instincts. Clear the ceiling, walls, and floor if you are in a building. When comfortable and in harmony with the room or land you have chosen, create the Wheel of Earth: mark the four directions on the floor or ground in some way that you can easily orient yourself. In your mind see the circle and the four directions. Imagine yourself in Heaven's Garden.

1. Carrying drum or gong, enter the circle from the east, where things begin. Place the drum or gong in the center. Set your intention.

2. Go to the east and face outward; double-clap your hands, and call the Dragon.

Dragon Invocation for the East

Enter, Dragon! Feet on earth, head in stars,
Come Wood, child of Water, food for Fire,
Come Spring, come Dawn,
Come Kindness, Banish Anger!

3. Cross the circle to the southwest, face outward, double-clap your hands, and call Phoenix.

Phoenix Invocation for the Southwest

Enter, Phoenix! Child of Fire, food for Metal,
Come Harvest, come Serenity,
Banish Worry!

4. Cross the circle to the north, face outward, double-clap your hands, and call Turtle and Deer.

Turtle and Deer Invocation for the North

Enter Turtle! Enter Deer!
Children of Metal, food for Wood,
Come Winter, Wisdom, and Gentleness,
Banish Impatience, Arrogance, Cruelty, and Hatred!

5. Cross the circle to the south, face outward, double-clap your hands, and call Firebird.

Firebird Invocation for the South

Enter, Firebird! Child of Wood, food for Earth,
Come Summer, come Love,
Banish Grief, Sadness, and Despair!

6. Cross the circle to the west, face outward, double-clap your hands, and call Tiger.

Tiger Invocation for the West

Enter, Tiger! Child of Earth, mother of Water,
Come Fall, come Courage,
Banish Anger!

7. Go to the center, turn your face and hands toward the earth, and call Phoenix again.

Phoenix Invocation for the Center

Phoenix rise from Earth to Heaven,
Come Fire, come Ash, nourish Earth
Come above, come below, come within!

8. Extend your arms and spin counterclockwise in the center nine times. Run clockwise in an outward spiral for three and a half circuits, while beating a drum or gong, then return to the center.

Now the medicine Wheel of Earth is open, the space is cleared above, below, and within a sealed chamber.

9. From the center, make dedications to the spirits of place, acknowledging their supremacy and offering thanks for allowing the medicine wheel. It is important for you to make your own personal dedication deeply and sincerely from your heart rather than mechanically reciting a formula: you can fool others, you can fool yourself, but you can't fool Spirit!

☸ Closing the Wheel of Earth

To close the wheel, run sunwise three circuits while drumming and then return to the mundane through the west gate. Or you can go on to create the Wheel of Heaven, the pakua.

🌀 *Creating the Wheel of Heaven*

1. With the Wheel of Earth in place, stand in the center. Have in hand a bell instead of a drum or gong.
2. Form the Pearl of Fusion (see chapter 4) and open the Three Thrusting Channels, connecting Heaven and Earth.*
3. From the center, face southeast and chant "Sun" to call the spirit of wind.
4. From the center, face the east and chant "Chen" to call the spirit of thunder.
5. Face northeast and chant "Ken" to call the mountain spirit.
6. Face north and chant "Kan" to call the water spirit.
7. Face northwest and chant "Chien" to call the spirit of heaven.
8. Face west and chant "Tui" to call the lake spirit.
9. Face southwest and chant "Kun" to call the earth spirit.
10. Face south and chant "Li" to call the fire spirit.
11. Spin counterclockwise, ringing the bell and chanting: "Sun—Chen—Ken—Kan—Chien—Tui—Kun—Li." Keep repeating the chant, ringing the bell, and spinning faster and faster until you are dizzy, collapsing, and going into trance or vision.

🌀 *Concluding the Practice*

1. Enter Heaven's Garden.
2. Go down to the Yellow Chamber.
3. Go down to the Purple Court.
4. Commune with Spirit.
5. Return to the mundane.
6. Close the circle.
7. Thank the spirits of place and restore the space!

---

*You can find complete directions for forming the Pearl of Fusion in *Fusion of the Five Elements* (Rochester, Vt.: Destiny Books, 2007). Complete directions for opening the Thrusting Channels appear in *Cosmic Fusion* (Rochester, Vt.: Destiny Books, 2007).

RESPECTING THE SPIRITS OF PLACE

We are fortunate to have a firsthand account of a shamanic practitioner seeking a site for a sweat lodge medicine wheel on what he thought was an uninhabited island in the Andaman Sea.

I walked to the end of the beach, toward a flat piece of land above tide level, about the size of a tennis court. The ground was more earthy than sandy, plants spreading out here and there and a few palm trees. After just one step into this area it was as if I had hit an invisible wall. I could not take a step further, although I still could see everything in front of me. I could not move forward. I found I could step backward, so could not be physically paralyzed. Again I ventured forward; again I was blocked. Was this another dimension? I backtracked again, took a few paces to the side, and tried again. No, I was not being allowed to seek sacred space in that location.

I spoke to Spirit, saying I accepted this. Then I was able to walk forward over the whole area without hindrance. I returned to the beach and cleared space for the sweat lodge on the sand, without intruding on the forbidden area. Next day a visiting fisherman told us that the land at the end of that beach had been used three generations before as burial ground for Muslim sea-gypsies. Spirit protected them to rest in peace.

Spirit has many ways of speaking and the shaman's task, privilege, and burden is to commune with Spirit.

The Wheel of Healing

Modern medicine might describe shamanic healing as a placebo effect, healing by suggestion. Suggestion can come from within, say by positive thinking, belief, or expectation, or from outside, by hypnosis, advertising, or ritual and ceremony. The shaman counts placebo as a healing resource.

Although in modern hypnotherapy the therapist is supposed to stay out of trance to better guide the patient, Richard Bandler, cocreator of Neurolinguistic Programming, asserts the importance of entering the client's reality with, "If it's good enough for them, it's good enough for me."

A shaman enters trance to step lightly in all worlds, in any world, entering the reality of the patient or bringing the patient into a reality of healing. The shaman addresses Spirit as the consciousness of the patient, for it is the spirit of the patient that needs the healing rather than some external abstract.

In the application of shamanic healing the practitioner calls on his or her resources, creating power fields, summoning guides and totems. Many useful practices are described in detail in *Fusion of the Five Elements* and *Cosmic Healing*. Here we introduce additional ideas drawn from the Tao of the shaman, he who creates his own formulas for the healing of others. In using personal vision the Taoist shaman becomes a "Master of the Formula," a true Fang Shih.

THE HEALING CIRCLE

In days and lands where a person was defined by his or her place in the community, the participation of the community in healing emphasized the community's power to hold the energy. Each member played a part. Friends, relatives, and colleagues gathered for a regular occasion such as a sweat lodge or prayer circle, or a gathering directed by a shaman for individual or group healing.

Today, as in the past, always and in everything the shaman clears the space and calls on the spirits of place, of the community, and his own guides and totems. The following guidelines can be adapted for local custom or personal preference; they are offered as a guide to inspire rather than limit.

 ## Creating a Healing Circle

[In order to guide the members of the circle into trance, first have each member look to his or her neighbor on the left, then to the right, and then across to the member opposite. In this way each person identifies his or her own location in the circle in order to be able to recognize his or her place upon returning from trance. Then gather everyone's eyes and offer the following spoken guidance, allowing for a pause between each instruction:]

1. Place your left hand palm up on your neighbor's right knee, and your right hand palm down on your neighbor's open palm.
2. Squeeze lightly and imagine your left hand receiving and your right hand sending love around the circle.
3. Squeeze and pull up the perineum and breathe in, imagining the breath coming in to your left hand; as you breathe out, imagine the breath going out through your right hand around the circle.

[Run the rainbow around the circle by drawing attention to the following points of the body and their corresponding colors.]

4. Spiral your focus up through the following points of the body and their colors:

- Sacrum, red
- Door of Life, orange
- Solar Plexus, T11, yellow
- Heart, T5, green
- Throat, C7, blue.
- Mid-eyebrow, Jade Pillow, purple
- Crown, violet

5. Now focus above your crown to connect with the universe beyond the visible.
[*Chant:*]

> *White mountain, crystal lake*
> *Ancient healing forest*
> *Sun in the ocean, fire under water.*

6. Draw down the ultraviolet light of the universe into the center of the circle as a shaft of light.

Guiding the Healing

[*Now you are ready to guide the participants to imagine entering the center of the circle one by one to receive the healing of the circle.*]

1. In your mind's eye, look around you, see the faces around you, hear their thoughts, feel the love.
2. Let your mind go to that part of you that needs to heal. Focus the love of the circle around you onto and into that part, above, below, and within.
3. Visualize returning to your place in the circle. Open your eyes, look left and right to identify your neighbors, and across.

This practice can also be used to invite someone from outside to enter the circle and receive healing. First ask his permission for healing. At the end instruct him or her to leave. Another use for the circle is to create a group energy body.

SHAMANIC GUIDED MEDITATIONS

In our modern world, the mundane dimension of "now," it is not always the archaic, arcane, or esoteric that impacts our minds so much as the language of "now." The shaman might adapt, shape-shift, or simply change the language and technique to what is appropriate for the patient of the moment. This section introduces three ancient healing meditations translated into modern phraseology: Healing Affirmations for Mind, Body, Spirit; Forgiveness; and the Karmic Map.

 ## Healing Affirmations for Mind, Body, Spirit

You can use this practice to help your self or others. In it a Rainbow Meditation is used to guide a person to create Heaven's Garden, then to neutralize the negative and plant a seed of wellness. If you wish, you can make a recording of it and then play it back to guide your own meditation. It has five parts: Preparation; Going Down the Rainbow Steps; Creating Heaven's Garden; Affirmations of Mind, Body, and Spirit; and Return.

Adapt as appropriate when offering healing affirmations to the uninitiated.

Part 1: Preparation

[*Allowing time for each phrase to sink in, say the following:*]

Focus on the breath coming and going through your nose . . .

With your mind's eye, look in front of you and see the sun . . .

And know that she is always there giving you life and light . . .

Even if sometimes behind a cloud, even in the darkness of the night . . .

Shining and smiling on you, giving you life and light . . .

Keep your face always toward the sun and the shadows will fall behind you . . .

And now, breathe in the sunlight between your eyebrows . . .

Breathe in the sunshine and let it flood your whole being . . .

With your mind's eye, as you look inward and upward . . .

To a point at the top of your head . . .

To a point at the top of your head between your skull and your scalp . . .

That point between your skull and your scalp relaxes . . .

And softens . . .

And grows warm . . .

That warm, relaxing feeling flows down . . .

Relaxing your crown . . .

The back of your head and your temples . . .

Relaxing your forehead . . .

And now, relax between your eyebrows . . .

And the tiny muscles around your eyes . . .

Feel them grow soft, and relaxed . . .

Relax your cheeks, soften your jaw . . .

And release your neck . . . .

And now, as your neck and throat relax, the tiredness and tension drain away . . .

Relax your shoulders, the muscles soft and slack . . .

As you relax your back . . .

The muscles on either side of your spine relax . . .

Your chest . . .

Your belly . . .

Your hips and thighs become heavy . . .

Your legs, your knees, your ankles, your feet . . .

Relax . . .

[*Longish pause* . . .]

🌀 Part 2: Going Down the Rainbow Steps

Imagine a rainbow arching across the sky . . .

Look at the colors, then breathe all the way out; let your lungs empty . . .

Then as they relax let the new air flow in like a tide . . .

And as it flows in . . .

Think of the number seven and see the color red,

And mentally say:

"I prepare to relax body and mind . . .

A red world . . .

I am more relaxed than ever before . . ."

Let your breath come and go as you count seven breaths of red.
[*Pause for seven breaths . . .*]

Then breathe out all the way, let your lungs empty . . .

Then as they relax let the new air flow in like a tide . . .

And as it flows in . . .

Think of the number six and see the color orange . . .

Something orange . . .

This is your physical relaxation number, the color six . . .

With your mind's eye look inward and upward . . .

To a point at the top of your head, between your skull and your scalp . . .

And imagine it relax and grow warm . . .

And let that warm relaxing feeling spread down . . .

Relaxing your temples . . .

Your forehead . . .

And the tiny muscles around your eyes . . .

Relax your cheeks and your jaw . . .

Your neck and shoulders . . .

Your chest, back, and belly . . .

Feel your legs heavy and all the tension flow out . . .

Out of your feet . . .

Out of your toes . . .

Into the earth . . .

Let your breath come and go as you count six orange breaths.
[*Pause for six breaths . . .*]

Then breathe out all the way, let your lungs empty . . .

Then as they relax let the new air flow in like a tide . . .

And as it flows in . . .

Think of the number five and see the color yellow . . .

With your mind's eye . . .

Look in front of you . . .

And see the sun . . .

Breathe in the golden light . . .

Between your eyebrows . . .

Into the crystal room . . .

And then let that light fill your whole being . . .

And mentally say:

"I breathe in the sunshine . . ."

Let your breath come and go as you count five golden breaths.
[*Pause for five breaths . . .*]

Then breathe out all the way, let your lungs empty . . .

Then as they relax let the new air flow in like a tide . . .

And as it flows in . . .

Think of four . . .

And green . . .

And the ancient healing forest . . .

And mentally say:

"Green is the color of health . . .

And I am healthy . . ."

Let your breath come and go as you count four breaths of cleansing green.
[*Pause for four breaths . . .*]

Then breathe out all the way, let your lungs empty . . .

Then as they relax let the new air flow in like a tide . . .

And as it flows in . . .

See the number three . . .

And think of blue . . .

And mentally say:

"Blue is the color of love . . .

I love, and I am loved . . ."

See a flash of blue sky . . .

Let breath flow blue as you count to three.

[*Pause for three breaths* . . .]

Let breath flow slowly . . .

As you count to two . . .

And see purple . . .

All disappears into one, violet . . .

As you mentally say:

"I am now at the deepest and most inward level of my being, deeper and more inward than ever before . . ."

[*Longish pause* . . .]

🌀 *Part 3: Heaven's Garden*

In a few moments I will count from one to three . . .

On the count of three project your mind into a passive scene from nature . . .

A beautiful place of peace . . .

One . . .

[*Pause* . . .]

Two . . .

[*Pause* . . .]

Three . . .

[*Click fingers*]

See yourself there, in nature.
    See the colors and shapes and movements . . .
    Hear the sounds . . .
    Smell the fragrances . . .
    Feel the textures . . .
[*Pause* . . .]

Look around you, in front, to the sides, turn around . . .
    See what's there, touch and feel and hear . . .
    See yourself . . .
    See yourself in this beautiful place . . . .
    See yourself, relaxed and moving easily . . . .
    See yourself, comfortable and at ease . . .
[*Pause* . . .]

Look at the screen . . .
    Look at the bright screen in your place of peace . . .
    Look at the bright screen . . .
    See yourself on the screen . . . .
    And now . . .
[*Pause* . . .]

[*This next section only do once for a subject, in their first session,* **and never repeat it because repetition reinforces the negative they want to lose**]
As you step into the Tao of renewal and re-creation . . .
    Only you can know your full reality . . .
    Only you can know the changes you want to make . . .
    Only you know all your resources . . .
    You know your power . . .
    Reflect on what you want to change . . .
    Make a reflection . . .
    On the screen in your mind . . .
    And now, on that screen . . .
    See the changes you want to make . . .

See yourself as you are . . .
And see all that you want to change . . .
Show everything . . .
Everything you want to change . . .
Show it on that screen . . .
See yourself . . .
Watching yourself on the screen . . .
And seeing all that you want to change . . .
All that you want to lose . . .
All that you want to get rid of . . .
Look, examine, and note . . .
What you want to let go . . .
See everything . . .
Hide nothing . . .
All that's to go . . .
See it, clearly . . .
On the screen before you . . .
[*Pause for nine breaths* . . .]

And now!
Look at the screen,
And see, at the foot of the screen,
A pot of black paint and a brush,
And take up the brush in your hand,
And dip it in the black paint,
And paint the border of the screen in black,
Side, top, side, bottom!
And drop the brush and look at the screen with the black border,
And see the image you want to change,
And see at the foot of the screen,
A pot of red paint and a brush,
And take up the brush in your hand,
And dip it in the red paint,
And across the screen paint a red X from corner to corner!

Crossing out the negative image,

And drop the brush and look at the screen with the red X and the black border,

And at the foot of the screen see a lighter,

And take up the lighter in your hand,

And now set fire to the screen!

And watch it disappear in a flash of fire and smoke!

And see the ashes fall!

Onto the healing earth,

And into the healing water . . .

And dissolve . . .

[*Pause for three breaths . . .*]

[*This next section you do in every session:* **using these exact words**]

And now, you see [*Talk faster here*] a bright and shining screen with a beautiful golden border, and on that screen you see yourself, in all your shining beauty,

Yourself as you are, and as you desire to be

You see

Yourself

On the bright screen with the golden borders

Yourself

As you are and as you wish to be, the same

You see

Yourself

In all your shining beauty

Yourself as you are and be

You see

Your head is comfortable, relaxed, at ease upon your shoulders

Your vision perfect, your eyes so clear and bright

Your skin is clear, your bones are strong

Your nerves are tuned, and your muscles toned

You are in perfect health and in tune with life

And this is so

As you see yourself
In your garden
Looking at your screen
The screen of your mind
In your perfect place . . .
Feeling the textures . . .
Smelling the fragrances . . .
Hearing the sounds . . .
Seeing the colors of nature . . .
Seeing yourself there, in nature
Your perfect place,
where you can come any time,
to relax, to be safe . . .
To see yourself . . .
As you would be
And this is so!

[*No pause, lead straight on into next part*]

🌀 Part 4: Affirmations of Mind, Body, Spirit

Mentally make the following affirmations:

"I am continually thinking creative thoughts to bring me health and happiness and all I desire.

"I am using more and more of my mind every day and use it in such a special manner that I become more and more creative every day.

"I have full dominion and mastery over my mind at all levels of consciousness including the outer conscious levels.

"I am continually developing my faculties to improve the use of my mind.

"I improve the use of my mind that I may benefit humankind.

"And this is so!"

Continue affirming:

"I am continually thinking creative thoughts to keep me in perfect health and in tune with life.

"My head is comfortable, relaxed, and at ease on my shoulders.

"My vision perfect, my eyes so clear and bright.

"My heart is strong, my heartbeat sure, my pulse-rate steady and slow.

"My heart, lungs, liver, spleen, and kidneys function together perfectly and in harmony.

"My skin is clear, my bones are strong, my nerves are tuned, and my muscles toned.

"My blood is clean and my lungs are clear.

"I am in perfect health and in tune with life.

"And this is so!"

Continue with:

"I have the power to project my spirit into any kingdom on this earth to know what is going on, to help and to heal:

"The mineral kingdom with the power of attraction—inanimate matter;

"The vegetable kingdom with the power of response—plant life;

"The lower animal kingdom with the power of instinctive reaction;

"The higher animal kingdom with reproductive awareness and knowledge of the Tao.

"I believe in the Spirit of Tao, the common knowledge, the outer energy.

"I believe in myself, [*speak name*] my spirit in the Tao.

With the power to draw on the common knowledge and project the outer energy, I believe in myself, in the manifestation of my desires, health, and happiness.

"And this is so!"

[*Pause for twenty-seven breaths . . .*]

Part 5: The Return

And now . . .

And now . . .

And now, in a few moments I will count from 1 to 7 . . .

[*Little pause* . . .]

On the count of 7, open your eyes,

1–2–3.

[*Little pause* . . .]

Refreshed, relaxed, revitalized,

Your head comfortable, relaxed, and at ease upon your shoulders,

Your vision perfect, your eyes so clear and bright,

4–5.

[*Little pause* . . .]

Coming up slowly . . .

On the count of 7 open your eyes

[*Little pause* . . .]

in perfect health and in tune with life.

6–7.

[*Snap fingers*]

Open your eyes

and smile . . .

 ## Forgiveness of Self and Others

This beautiful and effective guided meditation is adapted from the "Calabash of Light," the Tao of healing of our Hawaiian cousins.

Each child is born of the rainbow and returns there at death. We are born perfect and gifted by the gods with a calabash of light to illuminate our way. In our passage through this life we dodge or embrace the slings and arrows of outrageous fortune; we give love, joy, and kindness. Each sadness, hurt, or wound given or received adds a pebble to the calabash, obscuring the light. Each joy removes a pebble, increasing our radiance. When our time comes to step back upon the rainbow, the more light radiating from our calabash, the sooner we can find our way home.

[*Pause . . .*]

Take your mind back to one day last week, to any random hour that you spent doing anything that involved another person or other people. You might have been sitting with a friend (did you listen or talk?), or buying a pair of shoes (or taking them back), or attending a business meeting, a family meal (did anyone argue?) in a restaurant (did you leave a tip?), a date (were you starting, continuing, or ending a relationship?).

[*Pause . . .*]

Take just one hour.

Reflect on what you did in that hour.

What you said.

What was said to you.

What you heard.

How were you were affected by what you heard?

How were others were affected by what you said?

What thoughts arose in that hour?

What were their causes and effects?

What do you think were the effects of your interactions?

[*Pause . . .*]

Let your mind dwell upon the images arising from this reflection on that hour, your clearest memories of this hour and your thoughts about it.

This is just one hour of your life. Reflect now on:

The thought that came up most strongly or most often in that hour.

Thoughts that came up most strongly or most often that day.

Thoughts that come up most strongly or most often every day.

Thoughts that come up most often or most strongly in your life.

What is the best thing that ever happened to you?

What is the best thing you ever did for someone else?

What is the biggest hurt that ever happened to you?

What is the biggest hurt you ever gave someone?

In your day-to-day life, what do you find yourself mostly thinking about?

[*Pause . . .*]

Suspend any self-judgment or conclusions arising from your reflections. Think back again, to the biggest hurt that ever happened to you, whatever it may have been. From that time, choose the worst hour you can remember.

Reflect on that hour, on what was said and done, how you and others were affected, the thoughts that arose, their causes and effects, your interactions with others.

[*Pause . . .*]

Let your mind dwell upon the images arising from this reflection on that hour, your clearest memories of this hour and your thoughts about it. Suspend any self-judgment or conclusions arising from your reflections.

[*Pause . . .*]

Think back, now, to the biggest hurt you ever gave someone. Choose an hour from that time. Reflect on that hour, on what was said and done, the images arising, your clearest memories of this hour and your thoughts about it. Suspend any self-judgment or conclusions arising from your reflections.

[*Pause . . .*]

Take a moment now, to remember the best thing that ever happened to you. Choose an hour from that time. Reflect on that hour, on what was said and done, the images arising, your clearest memories of this hour and your thoughts about it. Suspend any self-judgment or conclusions arising from your reflections.

[*Pause . . .*]

And then, remember the best thing you ever did for someone else. Choose an hour from that time. Reflect on that hour, on what was said and done, the images arising, your clearest memories of this hour and your thoughts about it. Suspend any self-judgment or conclusions arising from your reflections.

[Pause . . .]

By your thoughts on the past and your responses in the present, you can put pebbles in or take them out of your calabash of light.

[Pause . . . continue to the Karmic Map, or end and save it for another session]

 ## The Karmic Map

Examining your karmic map, the connections of persons and events that have influenced your life, can explain origins and causes of your present thoughts and responses. But what is the whole story? Did you know what a stepgrandparent suffered as a child that influenced how she later treated her own, and how that chain of events might have affected your own childhood? If you did know what happened, you might not forgive but you would at least understand that whatever it was . . . IT WAS NOT YOUR FAULT!

And on deeper reflection it might not have been theirs, entirely, and who knows what might have caused the wrong in the first instance—except to understand that it was almost certainly not the first instance.

[Pause . . .]

You can remove the pebbles from the calabash. You can restore the light, for yourself and for them, all of them, for all time is now and the karmic connections are always.

[Pause . . .]

As a child you may have heard your parents talking about their grandfathers or grandmothers, who would have been among your eight great-grandparents. You may even have known them yourself. In many families these are the earliest relatives of whom you have conscious knowledge, directly or by hearsay. As above, so below: you may know your own great-grandchildren, or they will hear about you from their parents.

In the Tao we have seven generations in our karmic consciousness: three generations above, three below, and our sisters and brothers with us in the center. We have other family connections: parents' siblings (our uncles and aunts), stepparents, their siblings, children, and the generations above and below.

[*Pause* . . .]

Your karmic map also includes your connections of heart, soul, mind, body, sex, and love: spouses, lovers, one-night stands, friends, foes, colleagues, business associates, teachers, students, fellow students, and the person who caught your eye as you passed in the street or the subway.

[*Pause* . . .]

You will become especially aware, as you reflect on your map, of those who have done you wrong and those you have wronged, of those you especially love, and those who love you.

[*Pause* . . .]

Acknowledge your feelings about those you love but who have wronged you, and those you have wronged but who love you. Observe your response as they enter your consciousness.

[*Pause* . . .]

You need only be aware of your karmic field in this life because now is the manifestation of all lives, past, present, and future. Understanding yourself in this dimension can lead to clarity and freedom in all.

[*Pause* . . .]

Think of the hours that you thought about before, and all the hours of your life, and the hours of all the connected lives, and the lives that have gone before, and the thoughts that have directly or indirectly influenced your own present, day-to-day thoughts and responses.

[*Long pause* . . .]

Meditate upon the effect of other lives affecting each other. Understand the wrongs that were done to those who wronged you, understand what it was that made you do it when you wronged another. Understand the pebbles in your calabash of light.

Understand that when you were hurt, it was not your fault.

Understand that when you gave hurt, it was not your fault.

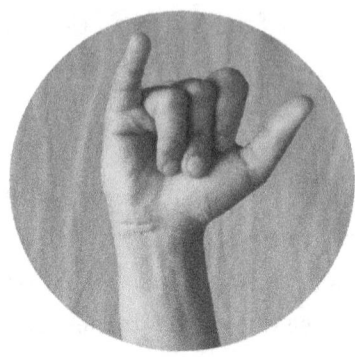

Fig. 11.1. Aloha mahalo, mahalo aloha.

Understand that it was not the fault of those who hurt you.

Understand that All Time is Now.

[*Little pause* . . .]

Speak aloud the words:

"IT'S NOT MY FAULT."

Repeat the words

"IT'S NOT MY FAULT."

Affirm the words

"IT'S NOT MY FAULT."

[*Pause* . . .]

And now you understand, you can cleanse your karma, be free of its conditioning in this life, and carry that freedom home, when it's time for you to step onto the rainbow with your calabash of light.

[*Pause* . . .]

In your mind's eye, visualize a person you love, one who has done good for you, or for whom you have done good. Smile at the person and say:

"THANK YOU, I LOVE YOU, I LOVE YOU, THANK YOU, THANK YOU, I LOVE YOU."

And as you recite these sacred words, you make the mudra pictured above.

Feel the love between you. Feel the light around you. Feel the clarity, and the freedom. You have removed a pebble.

[*Pause* . . .]

In your mind's eye, visualize someone you have hurt or wronged.

Visualize that person looking at you. See the expression in his or her eyes. Say to that one:

"IT'S NOT YOUR FAULT, IT'S NOT MY FAULT."

[*Pause . . .*]

And then repeat the mudra and the words: "THANK YOU, I LOVE YOU, I LOVE YOU, THANK YOU" again and again until the person smiles, and you feel the love, and you feel the light, and the clarity, and the freedom. And then, remove a pebble from your calabash of light. Bathe in brilliance.

[*Pause . . .*]

In your mind's eye, visualize someone who has hurt or wronged you. Visualize that person looking at you. See the expression in his or her eyes. Say to that one: "IT'S NOT YOUR FAULT, IT'S NOT MY FAULT," and then repeat the mudra and the words "THANK YOU, I LOVE YOU, I LOVE YOU, THANK YOU" until the person smiles, and you feel the love, and you feel the light, and the clarity, and the freedom. Remove a pebble from your calabash of light. Bathe in its radiance.

[*Pause . . .*]

It does not matter how long you spend on each person as long as you repeat the mudra and the words "THANK YOU, I LOVE YOU" until the person smiles and you feel the love, the light, the clarity, and the freedom, and, only then, remove another pebble and live in light.

[*Pause . . .*]

How many people? How many hours? This is a life path. When you step upon the rainbow, calabash clear of pebbles, you become the light!

AWAKENING HEALING LIGHT

Born or made, a shaman communes with Spirit. Each has his or her own way and some have a more intimate relationship than others. Each finds or is given resources for healing. In the Tao we learn special meditations and specific practices to awaken healing light, both for ourselves and for others. This awakening has been known to occur spontaneously. We are fortunate to have the following two independent eyewitness accounts of group healing by a shaman from another, similar, tradition who was himself awakened by healing light.

The first account is by a Taoist practitioner, Peng.

The shaman, a handsome middle-aged man with grey-streaked black hair, began by explaining how he had been called. "I was twenty years old, when I saw the light. Blinded by light, flung to the ground by an invisible force, I lay unconscious, I don't know how long. When I awoke to a circle of anxious faces I could see their thoughts. The light showed me their bones, muscles, and organs, and their energy fields. And I could shine the light upon them and heal them! My mission began. I created the prayers of healing, of forgiveness, of peace-making."

His gift became known and he healed across the land. I sat among some two hundred in an auditorium. The shaman told his story in the rich tones of South Carolina, moving around the stage in his easy way, talking to the audience so each felt "He's talking to me."

He said, "Hands up, anyone with back pain!" and two-thirds raised their hands. I did not, although feeling twinges and sometimes real discomfort that I put down to posture or not doing Spinal Cord Breathing as often as I should. The shaman raised his hand and snapped his fingers. In the ensuing astonished silence the audience looked around at each other.

"Hands up, all those still with back pain!"

Nobody moved.

That small quiet miracle woke me up. Ten years later, my back has stayed free of pain, the only time it hurts being when I've sat too long in lotus.

The second account is from the author Esther Jantzen, whom we thank for permission to reproduce her notes of what she recalled of the shaman's words.

You've got to do your life your way, doing what's best for you, what you feel like you should do. Get on your path and do it your way! What you desire gets to become yours. The Light always wants to give you what you want. Ask the Light to lead, guide, direct, and protect, and then we can be on autopilot—we don't have to think, we can just be.

Follow the feeling (not the emotion), but the feeling of your body. Chill the mental. Relax. Desire it, desire to know. Everyone knows the truth; it's in your heart, not your mind. It's wrong information that desire causes suffering: knowing comes when you follow your desire; a husband comes when you follow your desire—but not the type of desire that drives the self crazy—that's a different story.

The Light is the bestower of gifts, the Light is the cosmic parent. Think in terms of millions or billions, and you've got it. Prayers cleanse us. Clean up your lineage; make peace with everything; love everything; love yourself, too—and you find happiness. . . . When you stand up for creation, for the life of the earth, you find happiness. Happiness comes out of relationships—us with ourselves, us with others, us with creation.

Feeling is a way of being, a trait to follow, a way to success in the physical, with ease. Simplicity—simple people have one wire [easy to heal]; complex people have a million wires [take longer to heal, though there are shortcuts]; we've got to cleanse the complex. Simplify, simplify, simplify. Then make it simple again. Keep simplifying—it gives quality of life. Less is better—it makes what you do more powerful. If you do a million things, it's diffuse; one or two things—more powerful.

This planet is half a grain of sand on an endless beach. Be open. It's the biggest word for humanity. Always open. Open. When you're open, there's always more. Learning can be scary; new universes can be scary—it may take awhile for things to be accepted. [We've] got to get bigger, to stay open. When you love everything, it always listens to you.

Repeated experience by different practitioners led to the forming of tradition. In the Tao we are fortunate to have much written throughout the millennia. Reading and interpreting the classics has entertained scholars for the same millennia. At the end, we draw our own conclusions, and follow our own Tao.

The Taoist shaman does what works to awaken healing light.

Turning the
Wheel of Love

All human sexuality is sacred in the union of yang, the force of Heaven, with yin, the power of Earth. You can either pray 100,000 hours, or you can consciously use the medicine wheel to guide the sexual energy in the Microcosmic Orbit (also known as the Small Heavenly Cycle). The Dalai Lama, from the closely related Tibetan Buddhist tradition, says, "How can one experience spiritual orgasm unless one understands the physical orgasm?"*

Sacred sex fits between "pleasure sex" and "sexual alchemy." Pleasure sex is just what it says: sex for pleasure, fun, emotional fulfillment, and sensual gratification. In alchemical sex such feelings are considered to be a distraction from the main purpose. Sacred or spiritual sex blends the best of both: pleasure and sensual gratification are used to reach a peak state while retaining conscious awareness of your orgasm to connect with the Divine, the Immortal Tao.

The Wheel of Love practice enables the elevation of human sex from the mundane to the celestial. In the words of the Dalai Lama: "If the meditator applies certain meditative techniques it is possible to create opportunities for grasping the moment and consciously

---

*Quotes from the Dalai Lama in this chapter are from his book *Healing Anger: The Power of Patience from a Buddhist Perspective* (Ithaca, N.Y.: Snow Lion Publications, 1997).

generating the experience of subtle clear light . . . during the time of death, of deep sleep, and sexual climax."

Aspects of pleasure, spiritual, and alchemical practices overlap and it is for practitioners to develop their practice in their own way rather than enslaving themselves to dogma. Practices are for practitioners, not vice versa.

PREPARATION FOR THE WHEEL OF LOVE

Sacred sexual practice follows an appropriate period of physical, energetic, and spiritual training. In the past it was commonplace for a teacher to give general guidelines of time required to achieve accomplishment in different practices, from say a hundred days to ten years or more. Nowadays the individual is more recognized as having unique ancestry, karmic background, and, in this physical manifestation, genetic makeup, educational, emotional, and medical history, relationships, and outlook on life. While some, whose physical- and energy-bodies are open with clear channels, soft sinews, and relaxed muscles, may be ready within days or weeks, others may need months or perhaps years of preparation.

- **Physical preparation:** The human spine is the channel that, when erect, connects Heaven and Earth, from the sacrum (sacred bone) to the Jade Pillow (occiput). The ability to sit upright, cross-legged, avoids the distraction of physical discomfort during sacred sex practice. Cushions are recommended until partners become flexible enough, and are always useful for harmonizing differences in body size.
- **Energetic:** Participants practice Chi Kung to evoke their cellular memory of grounding, rooting, and centering. Tai Chi, with its spiraling forms replicating the double helix of our DNA, opens the meridians connecting the yang of Heaven with the yin of Earth.*

---

*Details of these practices can be found in *Golden Elixir Chi Kung* (Rochester, Vt.: Destiny Books, 2004) and *The Inner Structure of Tai Chi* (Rochester, Vt.: Destiny Books, 2005).

- **Spiritual:** Regular practice of the Microcosmic Orbit, Fusion practices, and the higher meditations facilitates the spiritual connection.*

Preparation is part of normal daily practice. In the way that a tennis player, for instance, will practice between matches, so an adept of Taoist Tantra will adopt a regimen of ongoing preparation, as well as preparing for each encounter.

The Wheel of Love Practice

The Wheel of Love practice has six parts: Dedication, Inner Smile Meditation, Opening the Channels, Yab Yum, Turning the Wheel, and Completion. Ideally practitioners work under the guidance of a teacher. Otherwise (and in sexual practice, however sacred, some prefer to be unsupervised) it is advisable to monitor the responses of body and mind. This is not to say that you should not push yourself a little—what muscle ever got stronger through ease and idleness? But it is important to observe yourself and any adverse reactions throughout the processes and to acknowledge those reactions.

Wise participants regularly check to confirm that they are in harmony with each other, especially when working together for the first time; if you and your practice partner are not in a preexisting relationship, be sure to agree on boundaries beforehand.

The following instructions can be adapted for use by an individual couple, though, as written, they describe group practice.

Positioning for the Lesser Wheel and Greater Wheel

In paired practice, sit quietly, facing each other with closed eyes, visualizing light within and around.

---

*For more on the Fusion practices, see chapters 3, 4, and 8, as well as *Fusion of the Five Elements* (Rochester, Vt.: Destiny Books, 2007) and *Cosmic Fusion* (Rochester, Vt.: Destiny Books, 2007); for more information on the higher level Kan and Li meditations see *The Taoist Soul Body: Harnessing the Power of Kan and Li* (Rochester, Vt.: Destiny Books, 2007).

In Lesser Wheel group practice sit in a circle, in yin/yang pairs.

In the Greater Wheel practice, nine pairs position themselves thus:

- Facilitating pair in the center—Wu Chi
- Three pairs form a triangle around the center—The Three Pure Ones
- Five pairs form a pentacle around the Triangle—Five Elements

This formation activates the spirit-energies of the One, the three treasures, five elements, eight forces, and the nine of completion.

🜨 Part 1: Dedication

Dedicate your surroundings and declare sacred space.* A simple guide is to have space around you where energy can flow and flower.

1. Thank the spirits of place, the yin of Mother Earth and the yang of Heaven, and any local spirits who may have an interest. None may have manifested there to your knowledge but it's a reasonable precaution to ask a blessing of whoever/whatever might be around.

2. Spend a moment reflecting on your karmic connections: spiritual sex is a powerful karmic cleanser. Let go of artificial perceptions of time past and future as you think about and thank your parents and your children, your ancestors and descendants.

3. Whether working solo, in partnership, or doing group work, agree upon a Higher Purpose to which to dedicate the practice, such as Spirit, the Tao, or a personal deity. Invite the presence of guardian spirits, tutelary guides, or totems.

4. Dedicate to each other.

Mindfulness is of the essence in sacred sex. (That's not to say

---

*See *Taoist Foreplay* (Rochester, Vt.: Destiny Books, 2010) for guidance on arranging a space for sexual practice.

there's anything wrong in a good old-fashioned bonk, but sacred sexuality is separate from everyday sex—this is this and that is that!)

🌀 Part 2: The Inner Smile Meditation

1. Smile inwardly, placing your hands to connect with your major organs, which look after your physiological systems as well as govern emotional states. Intention overrides anatomical precision.
2. Visualize your organs smiling back at you.
3. When you smile at your heart, think of love: love for yourself, love for the partner or group you are about to work with, love for all beings.
4. Smile at your lungs and contemplate courage, courage to do whatever you need to do.
5. Smiling at your liver, think of kindness and be thankful for the many opportunities you are given to forgive.
6. Smile at your spleen, representing the organs of nourishment, and feel serene.
7. When you smile at your kidneys, see them as guardians of your ancestral chi, the storehouse of your genetic energy, and be thankful for your wisdom.
8. And then place your hands on your sexual organ and smile as you thank it for its power of creation and the pleasure it can give, and understand pleasure as the gate to bliss, on the path to ecstasy, in all dimensions.

🌀 Part 3: Opening the Channels: Preliminary Movements and Breathing

Now face your partner, both seated, with eyes closed. Place one hand on your heart, the other on your genitals, aware of the connection between love and sex, fire and water, yin and yang, Dragon and Tiger. Begin a gentle massage of your heart and genitals as you sway slowly back and forth, breathing in gently as you lean backward, and releasing the breath out as you lean forward.

When the stirrings of arousal begin, cease the self-massage and clasp your hands together in front, left palm up, right palm down. Imagine your breath traveling up your back as you lean back, and down your front as you sway forward. Touch your tongue to the roof of your mouth.

1. Visualize a soft flow of liquid light, rising up your spine as you breathe in and lean back, flowing over your crown and down between your eyebrows, becoming liquid sweetness as it flows down with the release of your breath, down through your nasal cavities, falling like Heaven's Dew onto your tongue, cascading down the front of your body from throat to heart and solar plexus, down through your navel to the base of your being and then up the back again.

2. As this sweet, soft liquid light touches the base of your being, squeeze and pull up the perineum, situated between the genitals and the anus. Imagine you are creating a suction pump to circulate this light energy up your spine again, rocking back, breathing in and up, leaning forward, letting it flow down from the third eye.

3. Feel, imagine, or visualize this circulation within your being. Let the energy flow in the Microcosmic Orbit, up your back, down your front, around and around.

4. Now open your eyes and move toward your partner until your knees are touching. Place your left hand palm up on your partner's right knee, and cover your partner's left hand with your right palm.

5. Continue swaying back and forth, breathing in as you move back and out as you move forward, and fix your gaze on your partner's left eye. Maintain eye, hand, and knee contact.

6. When you both feel ready, which you can indicate by a glance, prepare to move into Yab Yum position.

☸ Part 4: Yab Yum (Maithuna, "Sexual Union")

Soft entry and hard withdrawal means Life,
Hard entry and soft withdrawal means Death.

What a nonpractitioner might refer to as "normal sex," with hard entry, ejaculation, and soft withdrawal, a Taoist adept might consider wasteful of the finite life force, a step toward the grave earlier than necessary.

In the Yab Yum position the yin partner moves onto the lap of the yang partner, as both keep their spines upright.

Partners will have agreed upon their penetration policy before beginning the practice:

• To go through the practice without penetration at any stage
• To allow penetration when both feel ready
• To begin with penetration on assuming the position

On first assuming the position, the male practitioner contains his energy, keeping the Jade Stalk (male sexual organ) soft. After sitting in Yab Yum and going through the practices described, Heaven's Dew lubricates the Golden Lotus (female sexual organ) and allows union as the Jade Stalk rises. It happens of itself through the positioning. At climax, the yin partner goes to full orgasm while the yang partner transforms the life force, which both recycle together.

☸ Forming the Wheel: Fusion of the Heavenly Cycles

As described in chapter 3, the Microcosmic Orbit (Small Heavenly Cycle) is the union of two meridians, the Yang Channel (Governor Channel) and Yin Channel (Functional or Conception Channel). The Yang Channel, also known as Du, left to its own devices, runs up the spine from the base of the body through the energy centers of the back, over the crown and down through the mid-eyebrow, and into the nasal cavity where, at the roof of the mouth, it flows inward and internally down the front of the spine, returning to the base of the body. There it connects with the Yin Channel, Ren, whose route is up the front of the body through the energy centers to the base of the tongue then, internally, down the front of the spine where, at the base, it completes the cycle by flowing into the Du and up the back again. The pattern, observed from the side, would be a figure-of-eight, or the infinity sign.

Connecting the tongue to the roof of the mouth forms a bridge between the Du and the Ren that bypasses the internal routes of both meridians. The yang of Du then overcomes the yin of Ren, reversing its direction of flow: down the front of the body. This reversal forms the Microcosmic Orbit in which the energy orbits the body up the back and down the front. It is comparable to a river being dammed in order to generate power, for this is the purpose of the practice. Beginners often feel hot in the early stages of practice, a result of "powering up" the energy: heat, as every schoolchild knows, is energy. The concept of energy can be easily understood when bills arrive for heating the home, or filling the gas tank of an internal combustion engine.

The Yab Yum position arranges the structure of two human beings to exchange energy by blending their Microcosmic Orbits into the Wheel of Love and connecting the energy centers through which the cycles flow. The result is to replicate in two bodies joined in sexual union the effect of the tongue connection in one body.

1. Place the soles of your feet together. **Women:** your soles should touch behind your partner's back. **Men:** your soles should touch behind your partner's buttocks.

2. To blend the energies of yin and yang, Dragon and Tiger, fire and water, heart love and sexual power:

   Men: Place your right hand on your partner's back, on the back of her heart center, between her shoulder blades. The right hand is the transmitter and sends the heart love of the woman down to her sacrum (the back of her sexual center, the Ovarian Palace), where you should place your left or receiving hand, to support her in position as she sits in your lap.

Women: Rest your right palm on your partner's sacrum, to transmit his sexual power up to his heart center where your receiving left hand clasps him between his shoulder blades.

3. Your sexual organs will be touching, connecting the base centers, ready to unite the fire of yang with the water of yin. In this position, Yab Yum, they manifest the mystery of fire under water, a secret formula of Inner Alchemy.

4. With your bellies connected from the pubic bone up, you will be linking your sexual centers (Ovarian Palace and Sperm Palace), navels, solar plexuses, and hearts.

5. Your throats are apart for it is through the throat that power over the other's spirit can be taken or inserted.

6. Gaze into your partner's left eye.

◕ Part 5: Turning the Wheel

Seal your lips around your partner's and connect your tongues, which will cause Heaven's Dew to fall and flow and overflow and spill down your touching skin and drip down your frontal centers to join Heaven's Dew below.

Breathe together, into each other's mouths and lungs, lips sealed against outside air. Exchange your breaths; let nothing in; breathe each other's life and live without air, as easily as a bumblebee flies.

1. **Women:** As you lean back, breathe in; breathe out as you lean forward. **Men:** As your partner leans back and breathes in, breathe out into her mouth. Follow her breath, breathing it in as she sways forward in your arms, breathing it out as she leans back.

2. Heaven's Dew flows as the Jade Stalk rises within, the sun in the ocean.

   Women: As you lean back and breathe in, you will draw your partner's yang within. **Men:** As you rock back and breathe in, you will draw in your partner's yin. In this way you will share your essence, your fluids, juices, energy, and love.

3. Keep your perineum squeezed tight, sealing the Gate of Life and Death to keep life within and death without.

4. Meditate with passion on the Wheel of Love, the union of yin and yang, Heaven and Earth.

5. As you lean and sway and rock and share, the flicker of arousal will spark the orgasmic fire and heat the water, and the rocking will quicken to thrusting and the thrusting to vibration. Embraced in bliss, grip each other, tongues locked, centers touching, muscles tight in backs, bellies, buttocks, and base (perineum).

6. Move your upper hands up to each other's Jade Pillow (base of the skull), fusing your energy centers of the middle eye that sees within. At this moment close your eyes, rolling them inward and upward to a point at the top of the head, between the skull and the scalp. Suddenly the cycle will change, and Heaven will open. Light will pour in, flooding your united channel from the center of the universe to the central sun.

All are One, in the Light, of the Light.

❷ Part 6: Completion

Keeping your spiritual focus internal, open your eyes and gaze into your partner's right eye as you very slowly:

1. Disconnect energy centers.

2. Disconnect hands.

3. Move apart except for knees touching.

4. Disconnect knees.

5. Disconnect all except the gaze, which you should hold until everything has settled and you feel yourself back in the mundane dimension.

6. Return to your original place, still holding the energy, focus inward, and thank spirits of place, the Tao, or whatever personal deities, guides, or angels you believe in.

7. Offer thanks to each other and all in the group.

 **Resources**

THE UNIVERSAL TAO TRAINING CENTER

The Tao Garden Resort and Training Center in northern Thailand is the home of Master Chia and serves as the worldwide headquarters for Universal Tao activities. This integrated wellness, holistic health, and training center is situated on eighty acres surrounded by the beautiful Himalayan foothills near the historic walled city of Chiang Mai. The serene setting includes flower and herb gardens ideal for meditation, open-air pavilions for practicing Chi Kung, and a health and fitness spa.

The center offers classes year round, as well as summer and winter retreats. It can accommodate two hundred students, and group leasing can be arranged. For information worldwide on courses, books, products, and other resources, see below.

Universal Healing Tao Center

274 Moo 7, Laung Nua, Doi Saket, Chiang Mai, 50220,
   Thailand
Tel: (66)(53) 921-200
E-mail: universaltao@universal-tao.com
Website: www.universal-tao.com

Tao Garden Health Spa & Resort
E-mail: reservations@tao-garden.com
Website: www.tao-garden.com

ZEN SHIATSU AND HEALING TAO

Universal Healing Tao UK
London Tao Center and Zen School of Shiatsu
68 Great Eastern Street
London EC2A 3JT, England, United Kingdom
Tel & Fax: (44) (0) 700 078 1195
E-mail: healingtao@btinternet.com

 **Bibliography**

Aoumiel, Ann Moura. *Dancing Shadows*. Woodbury, Minn.: Llewellyn, 1994.

———. *Green Witchcraft*. Woodbury, Minn.: Llewellyn, 1996.

Bates, Brian. *The Way of Wyrd*. London: Hay House, 2004.

Bouteloup, Guillaume. "Uses of the I Ching." Unpublished research paper, 2007.

Buck, Pearl. *The Good Earth*. New York: Pocket Books, 2005.

Carter, Forrest. *The Education of Little Tree*. Albuquerque: University of New Mexico Press, 2001.

Castaneda, Carlos. *Journey to Ixtlan*. New York: Penguin, 1975.

Chia, Mantak. *Bone Marrow Nei Kung*. Rochester, Vt.: Destiny Books, 2006.

———. *Cosmic Fusion*. Rochester, Vt.: Destiny Books, 2007.

———. *Fusion of the Eight Psychic Channels*. Rochester, Vt.: Destiny Books, 2009.

———. *Fusion of the Five Elements*. Rochester, Vt.: Destiny Books, 2007.

———. *Golden Elixir Chi Kung*. Rochester, Vt.: Destiny Books, 2004.

———. *Healing Light of the Tao*. Rochester, Vt.: Destiny Books, 2008.

———. *Healing Love through the Tao*. Rochester, Vt.: Destiny Books, 2005.

———. *The Inner Structure of Tai Chi*. Rochester, Vt.: Destiny Books, 2005.

———. *The Six Healing Sounds*. Rochester, Vt.: Destiny Books, 2007.

———. *Taoist Astral Healing*. Rochester, Vt.: Destiny Books, 2004.

———. *Taoist Cosmic Healing*. Rochester, Vt.: Destiny Books, 2003.

———. *The Taoist Soul Body: Harnessing the Power of Kan and Li*. Rochester, Vt.: Destiny Books, 2007.

Chia, Mantak, and Kris Deva North, *Taoist Foreplay*. Rochester, Vt.: Destiny Books, 2010.

Clausewitz, Carl von. *On War*. Cheshire, UK: Everyman, 1993.

Dalai Lama, The. *Healing Anger: The Power of Patience from a Buddhist Perspective*. Translated by Geshe Thupten Jinpa. Ithaca, N.Y.: Snow Lion Publications, 1997.

Eggerton, John Mark. "Calling the Directions." Self-published by the author. San Francisco, 2007.

Eliade, Mircea. *Shamanism: Archaic Techniques of Ecstasy*. Princeton, N.J.: Princeton University Press, 1970.

Ellis, Normandi. *Awakening Osiris*. Grand Rapids, Mich.: Phanes Press, 1994.

Herne, Richard. *Magic Shamanism Taoism*. Woodbury, Minn.: Llewellyn, 2001.

Jantzen, Esther. "Meeting Howard Wills," blog (May 23, 2008). http://www.estherjantzen.wordpress.com.

Jarrett, Lonny S. *Nourishing Destiny*. Stockbridge, Mass.: Spirit Path Press, 1999.

Kaiguo, Chen, and Zheng Shunchao. *Opening the Dragon Gate: The Making of a Modern Tao Wizard*. Translated by Thomas Cleary. North Clarendon, Vt.: Tuttle Publishing, 1998.

Kharitidi, Olga. *Entering the Circle*. New York: Thorsons, 1998.

Kohn, Livia. *The Taoist Experience*. Albany: State University of New York Press, 1993.

Lao Tzu. *Tao Te Ching*. Translated by John C. H. Wu. New York: St. Johns University Press, 1961.

Lawlor, Robert. *Voices of the First Day*. Rochester, Vt.: Inner Traditions, 1991.

Matsumoto, Kiiko, and Stephen Birch. *Hara Diagnosis: Reflections on the Sea*. London: Churchill Livingstone, 1993.

Nichols, Ross. *The Book of Druidry*. Reprint ed. New York: Thorsons, 1992.

North, Kris Deva. *Finding Spirit*. London: Universal Tao Publications, 2006.

——. "Calabash of Light." *Positive Health* 91 (August 2003).

Ouspensky, P. D. *In Search of the Miraculous.* London: Arkana, 1988.

Pennick, Nigel. *Practical Magic in the Northern Tradition.* Loughborough, U.K.: Thoth Publications, 1994.

Pullman, Philip. *His Dark Materials.* New York: Scholastic, 2007.

Robinet, Isabelle. *Taoist Meditation.* Albany: State University of New York Press, 1993.

Sams, Jamie, and David Carson. *Medicine Cards.* New York: Saint Martin's Press, 1999.

Schipper, Kristofer. *The Taoist Body.* Berkeley: University of California Press, 1994.

Storm, Hyemeyohsts. *Lightningbolt.* New York: Thorsons, 1997.

Trungpa, Chogyam. *Shambhala: The Sacred Path of the Warrior.* Boston: Shambhala, 1996.

Vidal, Gore. *Creation.* New York: Ballantine, 1981.

Wile, Douglas. *Art of the Bedchamber.* Albany: State University of New York Press, 1992.

Winchester, Simon. *The River at the Centre of the World.* London: Penguin, 1998.

Wong, Eva. *The Shambhala Guide to Taoism.* Boston: Shambhala, 1996.

About the Authors

MANTAK CHIA

Mantak Chia has been studying the Taoist approach to life since childhood. His mastery of this ancient knowledge, enhanced by his study of other disciplines, has resulted in the development of the Universal Tao System, which is now being taught throughout the world.

Mantak Chia was born in Thailand to Chinese parents in 1944. When he was six years old, he learned from Buddhist monks how to sit and "still the mind." While in grammar school he learned traditional Thai boxing, and soon went on to acquire considerable skill in Aikido, Yoga, and Tai Chi. His studies of the Taoist way of life began in earnest when he was a student in Hong Kong, ultimately leading to his mastery of a wide variety of esoteric disciplines, with the guidance of several masters, including Master I Yun, Master Meugi, Master Cheng Yao Lun, and Master Pan Yu. To better understand the mechanisms behind healing energy, he also studied Western anatomy and medical sciences.

Master Chia has taught his system of healing and energizing practices to tens of thousands of students and trained more than two thousand instructors and practitioners throughout the world. He has established centers for Taoist study and training in many countries around the globe. In June of 1990, he was honored by the International Congress of Chinese Medicine and Qi Gong (Chi Kung), which named him the Qi Gong Master of the Year.

KRIS DEVA NORTH

Master of the Zen School and Taoist Master-Trainer, Kris Deva North has been involved in healing meditation since 1972 and Taoist practice since 1987. In 1993 he cofounded the Zen School of Shiatsu and London Universal Healing Tao Centre.

As the UK representative of the Taoist Master Mantak Chia, Kris integrates shamanic, tantric, and Taoist traditions with modern life-training techniques, from Mind Dynamics of the 1970s to neurolinguistic programming of the new millennium. His experiences range from living with Kali worshippers of Nepal to traveling with a Thai Buddhist monk; from satsang with Shiva sadhus in the Himalaya to study with shamans of Africa, North America, and Hawaii; learning with Aboriginal men of high degree in Australia to darshan with the Dalai Lama; and from witnessing last rites in Varanasi to puja with the Brahmins of Pushkar.

UK national TV appearances include: *Bliss*, Emma Freud's series on sex and religion; Nick Hancock's *Sex and Stopping: History of Contraception*; Carlton TV *City Survival Guide*; and Channel 4 *Extreme Celebrity Detox*.

With Mantak Chia, he is the coauthor of *Taoist Foreplay*. On his own he has published *Finding Spirit in Zen Shiatsu* and he is a featured contributor to the anthology *Bouncing Back—Thriving in Changing Times*. His published articles include "Zen as a Philosophical Discipline"; "Taoist Teaching, Taoist Practice, Taoist Life"; "Calabash of Light—Hawaiian Huna Healing"; and the definitive interview with Mantak Chia.

www.healing-tao.co.uk
www.learn-shiatsu.co.uk

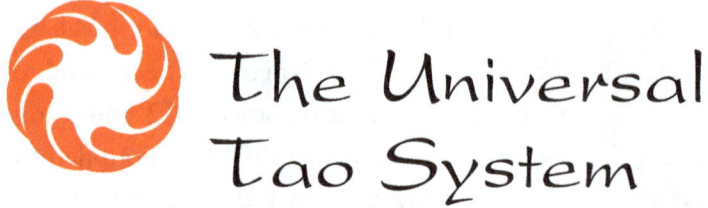

The Universal Tao System

The ultimate goal of Taoist practice is to transcend physical boundaries through the development of the soul and the spirit within the human. That is also the guiding principle behind the Universal Tao, a practical system of self-development that enables individuals to complete the harmonious evolution of their physical, mental, and spiritual bodies. Through a series of ancient Chinese meditative and internal energy exercises, the practitioner learns to increase physical energy, release tension, improve health, practice self-defense, and gain the ability to heal him- or herself and others. In the process of creating a solid foundation of health and well-being in the physical body, the practitioner also creates the basis for developing his or her spiritual potential by learning to tap into the natural energies of the sun, moon, earth, stars, and other environmental forces.

The Universal Tao practices are derived from ancient techniques rooted in the processes of nature. They have been gathered and integrated into a coherent, accessible system for well-being that works directly with the life force, or chi, that flows through the meridian system of the body.

Master Chia has spent years developing and perfecting techniques for teaching these traditional practices to students around the world through ongoing classes, workshops, private instruction, and healing sessions, as well as books and video and audio products. Further information can be obtained at **www.universal-tao.com.**

Good Chi • Good Heart • Good Intention

Index

Page numbers in *italics* refer to illustrations.

BOOKS OF RELATED INTEREST

Taoist Foreplay
Love Meridians and Pressure Points
by Mantak Chia and Kris Deva North

Taoist Cosmic Healing
Chi Kung Color Healing Principles for
Detoxification and Rejuvenation
by Mantak Chia

Living in the Tao
The Effortless Path of Self-Discovery
by Mantak Chia and William U. Wei

Sexual Reflexology
Activating the Taoist Points of Love
by Mantak Chia and William U. Wei

Healing Love through the Tao
Cultivating Female Sexual Energy
by Mantak Chia

The Alchemy of Sexual Energy
Connecting to the Universe from Within
by Mantak Chia

The Secret Teachings of the Tao Te Ching
by Mantak Chia and Tao Huang

Healing Light of the Tao
Foundational Practices to Awaken Chi Energy
by Mantak Chia

INNER TRADITIONS • BEAR & COMPANY
P.O. Box 388
Rochester, VT 05767
1-800-246-8648
www.InnerTraditions.com

Or contact your local bookseller